NOT FOR SAINTS

Leonardo Lojero

authorHOUSE®

AuthorHouse™
1663 Liberty Drive
Bloomington, IN 47403
www.authorhouse.com
Phone: 833-262-8899

Published by AuthorHouse 04/18/2022

ISBN: 978-1-6655-5745-0 (sc)
ISBN: 978-1-6655-5743-6 (hc)
ISBN: 978-1-6655-5744-3 (e)

Library of Congress Control Number: 2022907361

CONTENTS

ABOUT THE AUTHOR

Leonardo Lojero became aware of the real existence of Jesus late in his adult life; this realization took him on a journey of self-search and inner metamorphosis. A fierce battle began the never-ending good and bad where he writes about the important things that play in the spiritual life. His only and sincere wish is a genuine change and complete renovation of all of us, to heal and be at peace. Born and raised in Mexico City, from a humble family, he was seventeen years old when he emigrated to the United States where he lives and works as an electrician, a part-time writer, and a full-time self–education.

I would like to dedicate Not for Saints to my wife Maria for her support and understanding during the countless hours I spent writing and specially to my kids who inspire me to write and leave a small legacy for them to guide them, they have always been my greatest inspiration this book is dedicated to Nicole, Matthew, Jayleen and my little Isaiah, to my mother who was always my guidance, to my sisters Norma and Yazmin for their unconditional love, to my aunt Lupita who brought up my love for reading, thank you for giving me the gift of having you all in my life! And help me grow, especially for my greatest love Jesus who touched me and inspired me.

The saying is trustworthy and deserving of full acceptance that Christ Jesus came into the world to save sinners — of whom I am the worst.

1Timothy 1, 15

See how the flowers of the field grow.
They do not labor or spin.
Yet I tell you that not even Solomon in his entire splendor was dressed like one of these. Jesus. Matt6:25-34

THE LIGHT

If our greatest assets are given to us free, like our life, our feelings, freedom, intelligence, why do we worry so much? Why do we embrace suffering? Perhaps we lack a deep understanding of our great purpose, open your heart and follow me on this spiritual journey. The water was created to give us life and vitality, the flowers for their scent and beauty, bumblebees to pollinate and make honey, lions help keep the savanna's ecosystem so on, and we all have a purpose in life. When a seed falls on the fertile ground, the Universe conspires, to fertilize it, water the seed with rain and the Sunlight projects the energy on that seed, with given time the miracle of life starts to reveal. Life is a gift given to us when we are born, the seed is planted as the miracle of life starts its cycle, the whisper of life from our creator covers the entire planet, the Universe is lively, we happen to be part of this amazing party of life and color. Have you ever asked why you are alive? Why does your heart pump? What makes your heart function? We know by common sense everything needs some source of energy, fuel, a motor, or a mechanism to move, our heart needs an electric pulse to pump blood, where does the electric pulse come from? Your heartbeat is triggered by electrical impulses that travel down to a specific pathway through your heart: The impulse starts in a small bundle of specialized cells located in the right atrium; called the SA node. But what causes this node to generate electrical charges? Is just one of the trillion miracles of life we don't understand, that and all the engineering in every creature of everything our eyes can see, we do understand a car was invented an engineer created every aspect of it, totally, and if I say the car evolve from a cell by millions of years of evolution you will call me crazy and ignorant and yet this car was built with lots of work, trial and error but yet we may deny the greatest engineer of all, the architect of everything existing, our own human body is the most amazing example, instead of nuts and bolts our creator used cells and these cells are a world of their own, each one with a specific function, as well as intricate systems we could never understand to bond everything together and regenerate.

Is the wisdom, the whisper of God, the holy spirit inspiration on all the creatures of the Universe, it does his work everywhere just look around, you could try to find the reasoning behind everything, the science to the smallest particle of the Universe and yet, you would still be puzzle, you could find clues but never understand the entire process, to every single aspect of nature creation, we know things move, things work, many have a built-in timer for seasons, things happen and work with mathematical precision, If the planet was just a few inches too far life would not be possible if the Sun was a few inches too far or too close we could either burn or freeze, everything was made with mathematical precision.

Take the seed and put it on the ground, do you really know exactly what happens in it? What triggers life into it? And why some seeds don't get to grow and multiply, the algorithm inside every creature design and shape is beyond our understanding, if you happen to study the science behind and decipher the process and design, perhaps one day after so much trial and error and hard work you may get to a point where the source, the light, the energy, the wisdom, the answer, is right there in your eyes but you just can't see it or understand it, the wisdom of God in everything created is beyond human intelligence.

For a computer to work many complex electronic components must be put together in such a specific and accurate form to work properly and perform complex tasks, a TV and every electronic device big and small that we use in our everyday world has a complex electronic circuit to work and many things inside the circuit must happen in perfect symphony in a micro-scale and we never really think about it, this world works the same way at a macro scale and mini-scale everything was engineered with mathematical precision, to work and make life possible in many ways shapes and forms.

It is not for us to understand a lot of things in this world but for the sake of general knowledge, study and perhaps exercising of the human brain a good understanding of the Universe is necessary if the reason for understanding would in any way contribute to the well been of other creatures and humanity as well. Then maybe our creator could help us find better and solid clues, when we have found deep discoveries many times we use them for our own destruction like nuclear power.

We generally seem to think we are the only ones on earth that can communicate efficiently, but who is to tell you that every creature on earth has a unique form of communicating that we as humans don't know, don't understand and are unaware of it, in that case we may be left out, if you ever watch the fiction movie Avatar our world can't be too far from this science fiction movie, in the sense that, the wind, the seasons, and all the waters around the world are in a symphony, composing and creating our complex world, where we don't take part of. The ever silence trees around the world, the plants and all the animals and insects, seem to know when danger is about to come, or when life comes back to the ground in spring and everything is a party of life. The order that was given from the beginning is at work all the time.

> And God said, "Let the earth sprout vegetation, plants yielding seed, and fruit trees bearing fruit in which is their seed, each according to its kind, on earth" and it was so. Genesis 1:11

When you abandon a piece of land or a home, nature would immediately starts taking over and in a few years everything would be takeover by nature, following the order it was given by the creator.

We are too arrogant to understand and admit intelligence beyond our complex brain but true intelligence is everywhere around, we as an independent been, are to learn by trial and error whereas in nature everything is hard wire to happen at is best, a tree is hard wire to grow as big as it possibly can, and on the other hand we only grow according to our personal experience and internal growth, by looking, through our parents teachings, the books we read, the media and other probably mistakenly grown humans, we pass on our believes, our perception and our little understanding of the Universe, as to say the blind leading the blind

Read (Matthew 15:14), For generations and generations; we come as visitors just like when we go camping we do everything possible to enjoy, eat, rest, and go through it knowingly one day we go home, but our trip here on earth is a little longer but definitely not to stay and also one day we'll go home.

Once a thought or an idea is embedded in our mind coming from our leaders, our examples, our guides, our love ones, we believe it so much, even if it was far from the true, far away from source of infinite intelligence, because our independence from the creator comes with a price, the price we pay everyday with the fact we have to learn everything on our own, this brings lots of anger, frustration, sadness, violence, hate, depression, greed and a self-center nature, and then you wonder why Some people are capable of doing wrong?, Is just the freedom of will, to do as we please good or bad, it does not mean that the infinite intelligence of God is not omnipresence, and omnipotent, is the freedom we have, to learn, to grow, to raise with all our learning and understanding, but when we distance from the infinite intelligence of our creator we are doom to be wrong, in pain, and a certain fall over and over. In the beginning the first men on earth, divorced from the infinite intelligence of our creator, we did what we do best disobey, and after all, we became travelers without guidance; but Jesus came to give us the message of salvation, to return to what we lost so long ago; he is never too far out of reach for those who search, those who knock, those who ask, he is merciful and waiting for each one of us to remarry our creator, how do we understand his word? How do we get to know him? One way to start is to read the bible as Paul the apostle once said all the scripture in his time which is the old testament today, was inspiration of God, for me it took me over forty years before I open it and read it for the first time, but I am glad I did, as I learn how much love there is for us, even when we don't deserve it, with this book I hope and pray you get many reasons to believe and many others to never give up, many more to understand your mission and a better understanding of the many whys we never cease to ask, I pray you get to finish because that something you need, you may find it perhaps at the very end, all I ask is to open your heart and go slow,

;" Don't you believe that I am in the Father, and that the Father is in me? The words I say to you are not just my own. Rather, it is the Father, living in me, who is doing his work. Believe me when I say that I am in the Father and the Father is in me; or at least believe on the evidence of the miracles themselves. On that day you will realize that I am in my Father, and you are in me, and I am in you.'" (John 14:9-11, 20).

there is only two choices either you believe or you don't, there is not middle or options to choose there is not warm, is either hot or cold, black or white, to believe some things he said but discard others, is contradicting, to accept some of his words and some others don't, is simple either Jesus was a liar or he was very honest, because we only accept a part of his message or we adjust it to our convenience, this unfortunately happens to often, we crash with his words and we find a way around them to accommodate what we want to believe and with that there is another point I would like to add where science and faith crash.

There is the theory of evolution where in desperation for an answer without a God comes supposition, insects, animals and humans may evolve and change over the years due to weather and many other ambient factors to be able to survive, like if a few generations of humans grow inside dark caves perhaps they would become very sensitive to light, develop perhaps a better sense of hearing, and many other things, the same way dogs have evolve to be domesticated and different breeds yes this kind of evolution is true but a worm evolves into a larvae then an insect into an animal and into a human this evolution has not solution and will never have one, because we know the hidden truth, there is a God; many things can be difficult to understand before we hear the message from Jesus, but after we grasp and understand, many things in our life become simple, until we understand there is a soul, a spirit which gives life and a God who gives the spirit, before this awareness we let our basic instincts take over, without the awareness of the spirit our actions can bring pain negative feelings, resentment, sadness tears and blood, and we create our own reality. We accommodate things and thoughts with creativity a fake reality we build with solid thinking where if it wasn't with the help of our creator and his intervention we would never bring down those walls of ignorance.

A flower leans towards the Sun, seeking its energy and light, to grow, that's just what nature do, but we are free, and much like flowers humanity is looking for truth, for light, but unlike the flower witch absorbs and accepts the light and energy, humanity rejects the light, to receive the energy, to grow and enrich the spirit.

This spirit is what gives life to these bones and muscles as the book of the Prophet Ezekiel- 37 describes, it is incomprehensible for us, is just beyond all reasoning, but the spirit is the life, it is what we truly are. Even if we can understand complex things, as long as we understand the message of love and the fact that we are good people striving to survive; we are just ignorant to the deep secrets of God and we made some mistakes, for as long as we live we have the opportunity to amend our past and become much better, while we are alive, there is always hope. many times despite the understanding of Universal love, to love one another, we do just the opposite with one another, when we said the wrong thing to our kids, our spouses, our coworkers and estrangers as well, when we get angry if things don't work our way, or when people think different from our point of view, or when someone is different from us because of the clothes they wear or the language they speak; when we don't put on the other people shoe, to see why? they do what they do, perhaps if we put on other people shoes, we would probably be much worst in the same circumstances, or when we think we are better more intelligent more attractive or have a feeling of superiority because the job we do and the things we own, or the color of our skin during those times we are rejecting the light because everything that causes division, separation, hate, cannot come from God, we are just rejecting the light, not knowing is in our own benefit to love and we instead continue hardening our hearts.

> "I am the vine; you are the branches. If you remain in me and I in you, you will bear much fruit; apart from me, you can do nothing. If you do not remain in me, you are like a branch that is thrown away and withers; such branches are picked up, thrown into the fire, and burned. -John15: 5-7

Now more than ever we need more and more love the lack of love especially inside our homes grows like cancer and the lack of love with everyone we come in contact is destroying us, in tsunami waves, our norms are "an eye for an eye" we are in a self-destructive mode all the time, our hearts are becoming solid rock, now more than ever in history we need love, we are living perhaps in the darkest ages, there is so much evil and cold hearted people today and we are so much used to it, we could live together and so distance, zero tolerance to not one, we need to awake, we need the light, do it for your kids the new generations.

The understanding about the kingdom of the light became obvious after Jesus reveled many secrets of our creator, but for many of us it is still very difficult to comprehend, why do we have to be docile and meek when the world does not work like that, the world demands us to be tough, and this is why his message is so radical and demands true change and hard work within, but when we start, if we do, we will not be alone, we cannot do real change without help from above, when we read the scripture, the word of God starts working, for one reason his word is alive and forever present it really has the power to move us inside in to real change, is an opportunity, a door to a new life, regardless of how we have live our life until now, what we have wanted and what we wish for perhaps is not necessarily good for us, If all of our wishes and thoughts became a reality they would probably cause us harm, or to others, and if we are prompt to judge, to point the first fingers, we are rejecting the light too, because we are too narrow in our judgment to understand other people's circumstances and if we carry on like we always been we are heading to a crash, but there is always a better plan if we make the decision to change for the better, if we want to find out if we need change here is a clue; the gospel says,

> "If your heart doesn't condemn you then have confidence before God". 1 John 3:21

When our consciousness is not at peace is a sign that we are not doing the right thing or that we have already done something our conscious dictate is bad, in such a state we cannot have confidence in God, and many times we just ignore our conscious, we silence it by forgetting about it and pretend it's not there, that's how we reject the light; it's our freedom to do it, our choice to be in the dark. Read John 3:20

To receive the energy, to grow and enrich the spirit is to acknowledge a higher being, one intelligence, a greater power, who was the engineer and architect of all things possible visible and invisible because it is on the day we acknowledge God is real we start changing or we become aware of all the wrong we been doing and we realize we cannot keep going on like that, this awareness is the awaking of the spirit and this spirit by nature has a compass and is looking just for one direction "heaven" and since Jesus said Nothing impure will ever enter it, nor will anyone who does what is shameful or deceitful, then we start questioning our behavior in every direction, this is good because even if we feel bad and ashamed of our actions it means we trigger the spark to enlighten a better life, this realization would never have been possible if we kept our conscious dormant. We all know about infrared and ultraviolet rays or the dark holes in the Universe but our eyes can't see them, yet we know they have energy and exist; this is just a small proof of the always invisible Universe we are not even aware of because we can't see it. And the emptiness in the Universe is a lot greater than the material world, then the invisible must be a whole and immense world as well; thus the things we can't see must be greater.

Just because we have created a world of comfort and pleasure and we communicate and move around the world with ease, we think we understand how physics and other natural laws work, we might fly to mars, create flying cars and smart robots but the truth is, we are only lightly touching and understanding the complexity of our Universe and the deepest of our human intelligence, many of us think we are self-sufficient and independent from a higher been but we are not, we are not at all independent and self-sufficient as all of our needs depend on our planet and we don't have any control of it at all, men is just another creature in the vast universe but a very important creature, as we have the privilege to be called sons of God, after we get baptized. And this statement fills me up with rejoice, it is undeserved grace.

To accept the light is to love and accept your existence with gratitude, to live your life in peace, do the right thing, think always positive expect the best even in the worst circumstances, have confidence and trust in God, bless all the people around you at all times even those who hurt you, stay calm at all times possible, this for me is still a fight, I have improve substantially but I still require lots of work, but all our weakness are good for one reason to make us humble as if we were able to conquer all of our defects we might get infected with pride and ego, we would never get to be perfect but with one day at a time we might be able to conquer the majority of our life to account x amount of days on the positive and very few in the negative if we fall short one day in our pursuit to be better there is always another new day in the morning, we must pursuit our happiness, whatever your idea of happiness you think is, but I believe for us to find it, you should find the things you love to do and go for them, for someone who loves to play basketball pursuing that would be happiness, and even if you don't make it big, if you love to play, whenever you run in to downs hills in your life you would find happiness playing, and this is true for all of us we have to find what we really love and if we are lucky to make a living from it, this would be real happiness, true happiness does not mean we would be smiling and laughing all the time, neither is in the money as rich and poor suffer and have problems too, it is when you are at peace with in your heart and have love for yourself and everyone and the things you do, when you are content with a good attitude for life, possessions are just instruments to fulfill your existence, be aware that not everyone is going to understand or share your peace, don't allow other people to dump their garbage in to you, lots of people walk like garbage trucks just looking for someone to dump their load in to, keep your lid close and smile, bless them, and know inside yourself, your existence alone is a success, love is the key for everything we do, we are all craving for attention and Love, even when sometimes we use the wrong means to get them, walk away from noisy and aggressive people but don't judge them as we all grow at different times and different circumstances as our behaviors are a result of past experiences, we don't know the abuse, and what kind of ordeals some people go through in life, and you can't blame them when they don't really know any other way, they can't get out of it, there are many situations when keeping silence is a virtue, silence is not weakness is maturity, love is the key, as we all have the same needs and dreams, we are not so different as we might think we are at all, from one part of the planet to the other, we all look for shelter, food, and love.

We would never know everything or understand the power of love between us, even if you are living among real angels there would be many things that would not look good to your eyes because you don't understand the real substance of the things they do, and if you live among monsters our creator would probably want you to look at their actions with pity for a moment and don't stop too long to think about their actions leave them, pray and leave them, don't judge as our spiritual eye is way too immature to be a judge, there is a judge who sees inside everyone's heart everywhere and we lack the complete wisdom to even comprehend, how could we judge when our spiritual eye is blind how we could understand.

Love is the essence and main virtue, to the light to enrich the spirit to seek the wisdom only the supreme can provide, to accept the fact that everything you think you own or is in your possession is just borrowed including your body; your only possession is your thoughts, if you accept this truth with humility and peace you will acknowledge how insignificant is our struggle, our worry, and concerns, our obsession to material possessions and beauty.

The way we always seek Happiness is just an exciting flare that after we acquired what we crave for; eventually will dim until the flare is off, and then the cycle starts over again. This perception of happiness is wrong and absurd as we could never be satisfied because human ambition is like a black hole that can't ever be filled. For us is very difficult to understand this reasoning because whatever we see is what we want to get, our heart deceive us, if only we could see the real meaning of our entire and very short life, we run like goats heading to a cliff without control, we are always looking to satisfy our senses and at the same time always empty, we feel lonely and find not understanding, we reason some, and when we can't find the answers we go back to satisfy our senses again because at least in there we find some temporary relief from our long and lonely journey we crave for dopamine, we long for everything sensorial, we long for possessions, for power, and when we can't get it, we might get mad at God, we become terrible judges of our own, and since we have not place with the so call "winners" we grow more and more dissatisfied and sad, we become bitter and sour and our efforts are always frustrated with everyday life circumstances because with a bad attitude we get more of the same, we block our blessings with our attitude, not realizing gratitude opens the doors of abundance if we exercise humility, not until we start understanding that our attitude can change from a rainy day into an awesome day, the moment our attitude alone changes everything else changes too, and the negative can only live in those who make it host, this grim picture is not exaggerated but is a reality and a reality many, many live by choice.

Where are those ambitions of our ancestors? Where are those frustrations they lived with? Where are those troubles they had? Where are their illnesses? Where are the scandals they lived? Their sadness, the possessions, and their power if they had any, they are gone just like our entire little world would one day come to an end, and the next generation would follow.

We can only walk one day at a time, we can't eat all the berries in one seating, we don't need much but we want it all because our heart has an empty black hole, we need to understand once and for all, we are soon to leave, we are running every single day to our eternal departure, it could be today we are not just humans, we are spirits on a human body.

We need to fight for ground to get ahead, today not tomorrow, we need to learn more, play more, be at peace more often, run for our dreams today, all of us are expected to grow to achieve to be better but we cannot do it with bad attitude, we cannot go on destroying others for our wellbeing, we need to move forward but at the same time our spiritual growth has to go hand to hand with everything we do and everything we build, if we don't our achievements are going to taste sour because we forgot to grow inside, eventually we will be empty, this is why so many of us find relief in drugs and alcohol regardless of their success, not knowing we can find all the joy we want inside of us, if we feed our spirit properly it will provide us with strength to overcome all the hardships and problems that arrive, we would use the spirit as our guide, this same spirit would help us become better in those things that are really important, like our family our kids, our own personality and specially help us to keep our feet on the ground to realize how important we are and how minimal is the struggle, how short is our time, it seems like the time is always moving super-fast, many times we get to the end of a year and we are in shock how fast the time just slip by, everything happens so soon that so many times we feel a Deja vu sensation and we don't take in consideration is one year less of our life, this is why the awareness of the speed of time has to give us clarity to live with passion and treasure the worthwhile moments, it is my hope that my words awake your hunger for the spiritual and the love for life in general, and if they can move you to change it will be the work of the almighty, many times we forget the words but if we understand the idea it becomes a small seed planted that could grow like the mustard tree, we would be on our way to climb the mountain where the only obstacle is you, the spiritual change requires discipline and decision, don't expect to change fast, is ok to fail, time after time for as long as we don't give up. Have you ever visualized what the world would be without you? People will miss you a lot until they get used to it, and then we will only be a memory that slowly will fade, therefore why worry so much? Why suffer so much? Why are we obsessed with things that we can't take? Why so much struggle and sacrifice for the things that are not worth sacrificing why? My message and the best advice to you is to read the scripture to understand where are you going and why are you here; the rest would slowly fall in place through the clean words of wisdom you will find in there and if you get inspired to read the Bible while reading this book just go and read it, I can assure you, one parable of Jesus resumes this whole book. One thing we always forget to do is live the present time, we worry for the past for the future and in those vague thoughts our present slips from our fingers, the short visit to the park, and while we were there, we were somewhere else in our mind, when we take supper with our family where we start thinking too much about what went on at work and next thing you know dinner it's finish and we were not there, when our kids talk to us and our mind is not there at all, and the worst thing about it is that we don't even realize our life is in the present, is not the future, our life in the past is gone and would never come back again, is either we live the present and make good memories or we live like zombies in la la land inside our cell phones, always wondering about everything but not for what really is important, our present life, when you hug someone you love, take that hug and enjoy the moment treasure every moment, once yesterday is gone, is gone forever, I'm sure when we laying down in our last moments in life, we are not going to be longing for all the work we did, the many hours we put at work in first place and our family second, but I'm sure we will be longing for all those moments where we enjoy with the people we love, all those many gatherings and good memories, I'm certain we would not be thinking about work at all, And this has to make living the present top priority, loving a necessity that would always fulfill our memories and our heart, if you just take one thing from this book, take this:

"Live your life in the present moment and be there completely and entirely" "be grateful for everything and specially to be alive"

It is sad to see, everyone looking down at a cell phone is as if the world stop to exist and only that electronic device is the only window to the world, but in doing that we miss a lot of things, and we forget our surroundings and perhaps many important people in our life become invisible and our reality is only virtual.

The best memory is the one we make every day; even the most ordinary days have some good moments, if you are merry and hug your wife or husband at the end of a long day in bed just to comfort each other, or if you have kids and they came running to hug you after you come from work, or if you hug your mom or your dad for a moment, or if you have your pet seating on your lap comforting you, or if you enjoy a dinner with your kids, during those moments we have to take heart and mental pictures to enrich our present every day and treasure the moment.

There has been many times when I drive in the afternoon and I see the most amazing sunset, is like a picture perfect where the sky is full of amazing color and many times I wish I could retain the moment for the longest time I immediately get my cell phone to capture the moment only to realize the picture on the phone does not even get close to the real feeling of the majestic view, it captures something far and vague from the real thing, many others I see the moon, it almost feels like we can reach it if we drive some more, it looks so big and bright and my reaction is the same try to capture the moment but in my cell phone the moon looks so far in the distance and not bright at all, is disappointing but just like that, many times in life there are many things we would only be able to enjoy in real life and if we don't we might miss out many of the gifts and blessings we get every day, if we turn away from our cell phone for long periods of time I can assure you, we would not miss out anything, but it would make you more in control of yourself now a days is the other way around the machine is in control and before we know the day is over and our existence was wasted in a virtual world

Where is this going to take us? To take decisions based on virtual pollution, based on subliminal messages the power of propaganda was used by Hitler to influence many intelligent people, nowadays the power of a cell phone to influence and move is very dangerous if we don't feed the spirit and if we don't take serious breaks from the use we make of it unless you utilize your cell to work, to read books or to listen to books, or to feed your spirit and your mind, you might be wasting precious life and we might be potential poppets from powerful people, this is dangerous times where if someone with enough power of persuasion could potentially move masses into anything, the less time people spend feeding the mind and the spirit the more vulnerable and prone to be directed by others; don't waste your time, our time is gold, our time is so precious and we so much take it for granted, use it wisely. The scripture says the strong live up to eighty and if we use that as an average and we subtract our present age what we have as result is the average life we have left, this is providing we are strong and we don't get any illness, many who have survived deadly accidents, see life as a precious gift and learn to treasure their love ones and many of life's everyday miracles, don't waste too much time on anything that is not helping you grow, do what you can while you are still strong and have the energy as this will decrease slowly because the day will come when you would want to, but you are either weak or too old, we go on rushing for the weekend not realizing is our life we are speeding we want to spend our time resting while we eat the minutes and the hours, how many times when someone we have loved or appreciate dies and then we think I wish I have called more often, I wish I have visited more often, this vane wishes hurt because we didn't utilize our time wisely, we all have twenty four hours but in the economy of the time many of us don't make good investments, we spend it the same way we spend every penny, if we spend our time in fruitless pursuits we are wasting precious life, if you ask any senior person how does it feel to be old they would tell you inside I feel like if time stop at my younger years but is on the outside where we find the reality of life, we age very quickly, kids grow, people change, everything is in a constant transformation, time is the commodity we use like an endless supply, do the math where have you spend the majority of your precious time and do the exercise to think of what you been doing with this your most valuable commodity.

There is a story where, there was an island where all the feelings lived: Happiness, Ambition, Sadness, Prudence, Precaution, Vanity, Anger, Wisdom, Richness, Love and all others; one day wisdom gathered everybody on the island and told them he had bad news, the bad news was, that the island was sinking and that everyone who doesn't prepare and build a boat would drown and disappear forever of the human nature, there was a big commotion and everyone asks wisdom, are you sure? There is no way, you… Perhaps you are wrong? Wisdom simply said I am wisdom and I don't make mistakes, as of tomorrow me and precaution already built a boat and we are sailing to another island, the next day they left, taking fear as a stowaway, everyone started building boats except Love, love walked around the island, the beach she loves so much, the trees she loves so much, love couldn't let go, as so much love was feeling for the island, the island was sinking little by little until one morning a big earthquake took most of the island and love realized she did not build a boat, Love decided to ask for help. She saw how vanity was leaving on a beautiful boat and love asked vanity, would you take me with you please? I didn't build a boat, Vanity said not I'm sorry you are just too small and your look would make my boat ugly, then Happiness was on another boat already leaving too, but when love asked, Happiness was just too happy to hear and left, then she saw a small boat, it was Sadness living, and when love asked, Sadness simply said, I'm sorry I am so sad that I prefer to sail alone, Richness was passing by Love in a grand boat. Love said, "Richness, can you take me with you? "Richness answered, "No, I can't. There is a lot of gold and silver in my boat. There is no place here for you." Then anger passes by and when love asks, anger simply said I don't want you here there is no place for you and me, Love was feeling despair when a very old man called to her and said you could sail with me, I will help you. So blessed and overjoyed she forgot to ask who he was, as soon as they were sailing a few minutes later the whole island sunk when they arrived at another island safely, the old man disappeared before she could say thanks, but then Love asked Wisdom who was the old man who helped me? Wisdom smiled and said "it was time," wisdom answered. "Time?" Asked love. But why did Time help me? "Wisdom smiled again and answered "because only Time is capable of understanding how valuable Love is, and Time will always be Love's best friend for the good and bad times.

Understanding from the moment we are born, to the moment we cease to exist every problem, every obstacle, every struggle was a lesson in disguise as our whole existence in this amazing place we call earth is a University, a school for our Spirit and where happiness could be possible only if we are born again within and if we are at peace with the Lord. How can I be happy? It is not as complex as we seem to think as the first step is to acknowledge your only possession is your thoughts thus detachment is essential to experience happiness at its fullest, when you are attached to possessions or people around you, the result would turn you miserable and sad, all the things we own if we love them like our house, our car our clothes, our business, and all the toys we have acquired during our lifetime, become our joy and happiness for some periods, and also with it, a sense of pride, nothing wrong with that, except the teacher of all times once said,

> For where your treasure is, there your heart will be also.
> *Matthew 6:21*

and all the material things we have are just instruments to help us navigate through life easy but we shall never love them; and when it comes to people if you love someone, and they share their journey with us, this significant other is with you because she or he choose so, therefore you can just give everything you have to offer in the relationship the very best in you and nothing more, don't expect the very same back, you just do your very best and is all you can do, if the person you love does not reciprocate the same, don't be resentful accept the fact that it would never be your way totally, when it comes to relationships, this is detachment, you cannot own people even if you have a certificate of marriage or if you have kids, if you think this way, you may be in for a lot of pain, our kids are a blessing and our greatest achievement, but they also came in to our life's as a blessing and not yours in fact, just under your supervision and responsibility where love is in the majority of people in its maximum expression.

And with all the people we love, we just share the journey a path where each one of us has to follow a different direction; we become attached to our parents because they care for us and love us, we learn to love them, just like we learn to love many of those who navigate the waters of life and many times we never realize, one day they would go, this becomes a very painful time where we grow as we do with all hardships.

Every creature on this planet require more than just two species mating, to come into existence; there is not a true understanding of the magic of human creation in the womb as besides fertilization there are amazing miracles we don't fully understand when the cells come into existence and start to multiply, the wisdom of God that creates any life form into existence, this miracle of life and light, imminent in all creation is a blessing given to many of us, at a certain point in our life's in the form of a precious child, the same way this light could be taken from us, I believe this might be the most painful and traumatic experience but the Holy Spirit creates, moves and changes everything, even if it is beyond any understanding, as we don't understand all the whys? in the Universe and everything that happens in and around our existence, our kids are individuals who have to follow a path of their own, you just don't own them, we must always remember and be aware of it, this is detachment, doesn't mean we don't love, perhaps this is where our love goes to the extreme, one way to love is to do everything possible for the people we love, to show your feelings when we have the opportunity, in the present, we have not control of so many circumstances in our journey of tomorrow, when you have a home and in one blink of an eye, one day you just don't, like in an earthquake, a tornado or our finances won't allow us to keep it anymore, when you have money, possessions and if one day you just don't, and all this material attachments are as well one of the most difficult, to detach, in this material society things are just that, "things" and come and go and we never really own them, as if you die tonight everything you where attach to, would be for others to enjoy, detachment is the beginning of happiness.

Read (1John 2:15)

When you have it, be grateful, bless it and enjoy it, make the best of it, as for every single thing that we do on this planet; there is always one last time. become resilient, Detachment can get you closer to your inner self, your core, the spirit, and precisely is in detachment where your prayer can be deeper as you acknowledge your insignificance in comparison with the Universe, we are like a small grain of sand and yet we are as important as the Sun, as life don't just happen to come into existence randomly, and the light where we came from is calling us back.

I particularly do imagine sometimes when I pray and close my eyes, I'm in a desert naked and empty, the same way I came to this world, the same way I would leave this world, I feel the emptiness, the wind, and the silence, the sense of detachment grows for me this way.

Our spirit has the key to understanding the wisdom, our true self in

17

the purest state when in silence, we must learn to listen, to put aside our everyday problems and worries stop having conversations within, and stop the noise around sometimes in your head, and just listen to those thoughts that come randomly, listen, and quiet your mind, whatever happens, to come in your thoughts write it down later or just remember it, I had some difficult questions answer this way, as it could have some significance and clues that could guide you later.

We live in a world with so much noise, distractions, and entertainment so silence is a luxury but it is essential for our growth and lots of times since we are so tired, that silence brings us to asleep, when we get opportunities to embrace silence, we should take them as this could be like a reset button to our brain, a cleanup from so much cluster.

The next step to happiness is to read or listen to books, to learn and don't just read any book, not all books are the same, we must read books that bring the very best of you, to self-improve your mind, your spirit, as for every book you read you stand a little taller each day, you might not realize in the beginning but reading and listening to audiobooks, would slowly start imprinting your mind with information and knowledge to reprogram our intoxicated mind.

Although we must be careful with books that make you want to believe you are God and you almost have superpowers within your mind, this kind of book inflates your ego and only pushes back where you don't want to be; alone and with no superpowers at all. Good self-improvement books should help you strive to be better without turning you, into an egocentric self-center one mind kind of guy, the best powers you could get are when you get on your knees and pray, the most fierce battles you would win are on your knees praying, the most permanent achievements happen when you are humble enough to be on your knees and pray.

When we were born our teachers our environment and circumstances would be determined by the place where we see this world for the first time, hence our ignorance and knowledge, we could be brought up with tons of good experiences and lots of bad experiences, those experiences, whether we're right or wrong they were implanted in the mind as seeds, our faith, morals, philosophy, education, our dogmas and behavior in everything we do, all of it was determined with a great percentage by the people who spend the first years of our life as our guides.

Our beloved parents took the enormous responsibility to raise us and help us grow, we might have forgotten they taught us a lot of things that mark every aspect of our life's today, no matter if they were ready or not they took the challenge with courage and for that, we owe to love them even more as if it wasn't for that decision to allow us to be here today, all the little world we have created would never have happened and come to exist, for that I applaud my mother and I'm forever grateful. Many, many souls are cut short from our creator plan, unfortunately, during these times.

Today we think our Lord doesn't have a plan for us even before we are born but if we pay attention to the scripture and we believe like the apostle Paul when he said

> *All Scripture is breathed out by God and profitable for teaching, for reproof, for correction, and for training in righteousness 2 Timothy 3, 16*

Then we should be certain our creator has a plan for us as is in the old scripture he said:

> *"Before I formed you in the womb I knew you, and before you were born I consecrated you, I appointed you a prophet to the nations" Jeremiah 1, 5*
>
> *And now the Lord says—he who formed me in the womb to be his servant to bring Jacob back to him and gather Israel to himself, for I am[a] honored in the eyes of the Lord and my God has been my strength—Isaiah 49, 5*

he said I knew you before you were born, this certainty is something we should always have in mind when a new life is created, and therefore never attempt to disrupt the plan our creator has for this new life; as if our children trash a freshly cook dinner without even trying it once, something we might have been cooking for a long time knowing if they only have tried they would like it, it is probably a bad example but I wanted to make a point of how much anger and frustration we could probably feel with our kids for trashing something we cooked with love not to mention a desire to punish them for their behavior, I could not imagine how our creator could feel when we cut short a new beginning and a new plan for another life.

Many times our early guides teachings, is the only learning experience and true teachers too many of us might have, for the rest of our life, the ones who built our footings, as role models to follow, as we become teenagers we use all those learning experiences, to build who we will be for our entire life and at the same time or maybe later on, we will get to influence our friends in the social life and our friends influence us as well, we then become parents and therefor have to start working hard to provide our families and to help them, we continue learning from the entertaining of a television, from the internet, from the media, from friends and coworkers, as we become adults we think we know enough, just because we are capable of providing, capable of taking decisions, but in reality our mind is a cocktail of uncertainty, fear, anger, resentment, sadness, and whatever other things the person feed his mind of the everyday things, past and present experiences and on the other hand, they might be others who go to college span their horizon with a college education a practical education but not wisdom at all and learn from the many things they do after work and the everyday life, they simply stop learning for the same reason, they are capable of providing, of becoming parents, they are able to take decisions but their only true guides that embedded some wisdom were those of their first years, those who built our footings, the rest was just practical education that fill many gaps to make sense of the world, we, like it or not, have a lot of teachings inside our head from our parents than we would like.

Our philosophy is poor and the cocktail recipe is the same, as whatever we feed our mind of every day, is what would influence our kids and all the people around. And there is nothing worse than being ignorant by choice and living in the dark by option.

A good example of this is when I learn about this Lawyer in NY insulting two women who spoke Spanish who were minding their own business, this is a perfect example, as you would think someone with a college education and a career is much smarter but is not the case, wisdom is something very far from practical education, bigotry is complete ignorance and lack of wisdom, as there are so many lives in this planet and so many ways to live as there is sand on the beach. But where true wisdom comes from? Where does it come from? It is certainly a blessing, a gift like that can only come from above,

> *The fear of the LORD is the beginning of knowledge, but fools despise wisdom and instruction. Proverbs 1:7*
>
> *My goal is that they may be encouraged in heart and united in love, so that they may have the full riches of complete understanding, in order that they may know the mystery of God. Namely, CHRIST, 3 in whom are hidden all the treasures of wisdom and knowledge. Colossians 2:2-3*

A cocktail of misery is what the majority of us carry all alone, poor judgment is based on our blurry perception of what we know and usually is very limiting and with this narrow mind we go around building families and the worst part of it all we teach kids as they are white sheets of paper where we can write anything good or bad and once they grow is very difficult to reprogram it takes all of your mental energy, is like someone taught you early in your life two plus two is five not until you go to school and the teacher places four apples and you count, on that day you might be a little confuse and at the same time shock or mad because reality was presented in your face with facts but even if you don't like the truth and you despise it you will face it one day.

I know all this very well as this was exactly what happened to me, I had to reprogram my mind, my spirit, everything I knew and who I believe I was, I had to change, many times we fall into the mistake of believing we are who we are, and nothing and nobody can't change us, but this is an absolute lie, I believe for many years this wrong thinking; If they don't like me too bad, if they had their opinion of me so what, this arrogant and pathetic attitude kept me in the dark but it was because I didn't know any better, I kept myself ignorant as many of us do until we die. And ignorance is never a blessing, it creates a lot of hurdles in our lives, and prevent us from growing to full potential as the book of wisdom says the fear of God is the beginning of wisdom, and fear of God is always misunderstood as we tend to think he would punish as a mean God, but is not the case always, is fear of hurting his precious heart with our actions because if we love someone we don't want to hurt them, our creator loves us and like a good father knows what is best for us even if we can't understand, but his instruction is like the rails of a train we must follow to get where we need to be not necessarily where we want to be.

Who we are? Who? As each of us is brought up in life and all these factors and circumstances take a huge role in the equation, our experiences, conduct, ethics, values, behavior, and morals already imprinted in our mind, to be who we are, are accounted for; Are we corrupt? Not necessarily, we as humans in history have evolved and have gotten a true sense of right and wrong, our laws are based on that perception of truth but far from wisdom, true wisdom is an asset and a blessing we must find on our own and it is very essential, we must start searching, knocking, and asking, as it becomes the number two-step to true happiness.

We must be prepared to abandon our old teachings, our old philosophy, and our old perception of truth, Read (Ephesians 4:22-24).

Now more than ever before, we have access to amazing great information and knowledge readily available, hundreds of people devote their lives to faith, the search and discovery of the mind, self-improvement, spirit, and behavior, our access to wisdom is not far out of reach during this amazing times, the bible is not just a spiritual book it is practical and philosophical, a road map to understanding not just the human mind and behavior under any circumstances but if you want abundance the map is there as well, a book rich of wisdom even if your perception of God is limited.

Many people have left the road maps they followed to achieve their success, their wisdom, and formulas for the abundance of all kinds, they left the legacy in a book for us to find, to understand, to follow, to instruct and guide, people who accomplish great things in life are eager to share how they did it, so we could follow behind and experience a life full of abundance and blessings, If that is in part what you looking for, but that shouldn't be the only reason or you are already in the wrong track, and a sense of fulfillment, a sense of awareness to realize how great is the opportunity to be alive in this world, where once you start feeding your mind, like a baby is feeding with only liquids and start growing to eat baby food until he gets to eat solid food, just like that, our mind would expand, our ideas would grow, our blindness would slowly disappear, then circumstances would start to change; it is a choice to grow, is part of our freedom.

But are we free, when we have invisible but solid chains holding us, are you free? When your mind is full of worries and fears are you free? When you have a short spark and everyone makes you angry, are you free? When you are easy to judge and point fingers and you let other people's problems become yours, are you free? When you crave so much attention you have to publish every minute of your life and body on social media, are you free? When you are obsessed with anything harmful to you and or others; you are a slave of all these things, are you free? when you are embarrassed to show you are a Christian when you care about what others might think when you are against their perversities and wrongdoing but you keep silent because you fear you might be left out and be judged, or for false respect, many, many, things are our masters and owners, if you let them be your masters, wisdom might be your liberator.

When you go look for self-improvement or audiobook with real value and knowledge on YouTube for example, and you realize it just has three hundred views, but then look for something stupid and obscene it has a few million views. This just makes you wonder, where we are as a community, as a country. Be careful what you feed all of your senses of, for that which your eyes, ears, and all of your senses feed upon, create your reality, due to repetitive thinking.

Stop listening to music that has lyrics that are negative or offensive or destructive, stop watching movies that have so much violence and obscene material unless you are fully aware that those images won't in any way leave a print in your subconscious, stay away from horror material as this is one way to attract the unwanted, because it feeds on fear, those who live on fear would bow down to the enemy, for that witch your eyes, ears, and other senses feed upon are creating your reality, due to repetitive thinking, feed at all times with positive thinking, positive material, art love, beauty nature, happiness, inspiration, but most importantly with the word of God, as this word shall never return empty, it will always be like a seed, like fertilizer, and water, it will awake the holy spirit within, to reshape us…

So shall my word be that goes out from my mouth, it shall
not return to me empty, but it shall accomplish that which

> *I purpose, and shall succeed in the thing for which I sent it*
> Isaiah 55, 11

One can't never be too old or too young to learn, bless are those who at early times in life come across the wisdom and teachings of the Master and leave a footprint on their mind, to really make changes, how much I wish I learned many things early in my life, I would had prevented so many mistakes and pain, but not one really taught me enough to make an impact in my subconscious mind, to really make changes, I follow all the colors, all the noises, all the visual attraction, all the glitter that attracts millions of young people if not, ninety eight percent of them, that is why, for all adults is a huge responsibility to teach with example and then preaching, if not, all the young generations will continue to make the same mistakes over and over, just because we are too lazy, too ignorant, too busy and too selfish, if we really want to stop the evil we have to teach the good when we still can, we could teach a trick to an old dog but it would probably take a lot from the old dog to really learn. We don't realize kids and young people are still like sponges they absorb everything quick, most are mind open, like fertile ground for new seed to be planted, there is a shortage of laborers most of us are too self-absorb in our own little world and we don't really worry about this new generations, we have so much to worry about, but we need to put our two cents to help, because many of them are hungry for knowledge but not one seem to teach, even teachers at school who have an amazing opportunity to impact this youngsters are too lazy as well, and many times too concern about what others might think, whenever we have an opportunity to give a good advice to a young we should do it, I learn many are wide open to listen even more than if their parents would talk to them, is my experience many kids listen more when a stranger gives them a good advice, they don't answer back as they do with their parents they just listen, even if we think the message will be discarded, we never know how a simple word may have the power to change someone forever and if the message is positive and lifting, chances are they will remember; If we can influence our new young generations we would be planting good seed, and it would be God work to make the seed grow to become a plant and a tree, many times people who accomplish many big things in life have a story where someone impacted their life forever, we should always be prepared to plant a seed, I have, in some opportunities started talking I begin a little hesitating but once I do, I realize, I have all the attention although many times is not youngsters is adults, but if we ever get kids attention is an amazing opportunity.

We were born to learn until the day our spirit leaves this physical body, those who forget and stop learning and moving are doom to failure, in this life, a priority is to learn to control emotions, with lots of discipline, to feel anger, sadness, happiness, frustration, joy, love, pride, etc. to be able to control and channel this emotions properly is an enormous task because everything we do is a response to an emotion, but it's one of the main goals in our life, we are here to learn many limitations as well, to know, as strong, as intelligent, as rich, as you think you may be, you have limitations of all kind, every creature in this planet is full of limitations and to accept this true is part of gaining wisdom, but at the same time we might have powers we don't even know we have, it is a self-search and discover but there might be signs, in your life to follow, there is a natural instinct we should follow, the same way birds fly to the south when the cold weather is approaching, we have a natural compass built in to follow, whatever we were design to do in our life, if we don't we might never feel the sense of accomplishment, most powers and limitations are in direct proportion of the knowledge and wisdom we acquired and apply in our life. Knowledge is power; we heard this phrase our entire life, but why did so few dedicate their life or free time to the development of this power? Because the number of distractions. Distractions are part of the challenge we must get through, all this distractions are there to hurt us in the long run, to get the discipline to dedicate time to the one thing that could make real changes in our entire life, changes that could bring real joy and satisfaction, of all kind, changes that could help you understand others and be more sensible to other people suffering, as not one is immune to pain, to struggle, and adversity; and on the other hand if we just let ourselves go by, live day by day with no desire to learning and new teachings in your philosophy and we learn from whatever we get bombarded each day, from social media, to television and internet, we could become judgmental, full of criticism, full of wrong opinions, or in total ignorance, in the dark, with our decisions leading to bad actions and bad habits lead to base our direction on our small perception of knowledge or like a sail boat sailing to whatever winds are blowing up that day, and this can be energy drainers, this can bring fear, the sense of emptiness, and the biggest problem of it all, is that we bring this bad feelings home and at work, we could be smart at work and productive, provide to our family but the lack of wisdom can bring lots of pain, on the other hand we could take charge of our full potential, We could get Lots of frustration and discouragement in our families as our behavior is completely run by our toxic mind, and the really sad part of it all, a little kid is following our steps. This cycle goes on and on and then you wonder why so much division in the family, why do we make so many mistakes and never seem to end, why we hate so much, why we are always on the edge, or why there is so much racism, this is just examples of the things we inherit in our dysfunctional families.

The subconscious mind, the mind that is dictating our actions automatically by the repetition and memory of all our past experiences, its capacity is virtually unlimited. Is like if we were bitten by a dog and felt the pain as a little kid, as an adult you would probably forget but your subconscious mind would remain you when you see a dog and you will feel afraid for no reason, is always present, I remember one day when I was working at a food bank as an electrician and someone had the radio blasting, that day you could hear the music everywhere, this music was something I don't particularly care for, due to the amount of violence and subliminal messages is sending out, I never listen to this music, they play the songs over and over on the radio during the eight hour period I was there, I was minding my own business, just working, then I remember on the way home driving in silence as I tend to do lots of times, I was auto-magically singing a song they play over and over on the radio and I didn't even like it, after this experience I was scared as to how powerful repetition is in the subconscious mind, even if you think you are not listening, that's why commercials are so powerful, if I listen to it for another week I would probably robotically start doing what the lyrics said in the form of subconscious commands, this is why many experts on the self-improvement discipline always would tell you don't listen to the news as you would start believing the world is a scary and terrible place to live and that there are more bad people than there is good, as all this is a product of your subconscious mind, telling you how bad it is. I once heard a bomb makes more noise than a cuddle, but for every bomb, there are millions of cuddles every day, but bombs make good news and money to the media, and please don't get me wrong, information is important but we have to be selective and don't let the news get your emotions afloat if they do is time to switch the channel or turning off the television.

The subconscious mind is the place where we are most connected to God, the place where we receive our intuition messages, the frequency in the subconscious mind where we are close to our creator, he can hear and feel whatever we feel, and he knows what you need before you ask

Read (Matthew 6:8)

Our Lord heals our pain and calms our sorrows if we let him, but just like when we teach our kids a problem in math and we might feel frustrated when they can't solve it, we as adults know the answer and are eager to help but we just can't give them the answer, even after we do our best to explain, we know, that is best for him to understand it alone, just like that, our father knows what we need, we get what we need not what we want, and in most situations, our process of learning is a lot more complex than a math problem, as it may sometimes involve a lot of other people, circumstances and places, our father might give us a clue a hint and they may come, in the form of something you feel the gut feeling, this is why is very important to follow that instinct usually that's where your fortune, your love, your path to follow, to find the true meaning in your life is, with every experience we must always ask, what I am supposed to learn from this? A door that is closing down may be the beginning of the best opportunity in your life, a tragedy in disguise may be the best blessing, there is a story of a man who was traveling on a big vessel when they got caught up in a bad storm and the whole ship sunk, that men survive holding up to a big piece of the wreckage and ended up in a deserted island he was not trained or knew anything about survival, but he slowly started to learn to hunt and fish, all alone he spend months praying for his rescue, so many times he cried as the whole island was far away from the maritime routes, his chance of boats passing by, was very slight, after almost two years of loneliness and hardships, one day while he was fishing saw smoke coming from his shelter, he rushed to it, just to find everything he owned and everything he built in ashes, he cried and scream out loud; every day, I pray for your help! And this is what I get as an answer! He was angry and helpless, he felt sleep eventually, the next day a ship sent a boat to scout the deserted island, the men heard the noises and woke up, he ran to meet the sailors, when he was on board the ship he asks, why did you come to the island? They said we saw the smoke you made yesterday from miles away......

Our lord has his own time and way, to answer every prayer but I do know this, praying without ceasing, at every opportunity we get, would act as a shield and protection to the never-ending situations we may encounter, as the good Lord knows, only in trial is when we learn, then by prayer we could get the strength to continue, Don't discard the fact that everything you feel, say, do, or think, it's not been feel, hear, or seen by God the supreme intelligence, the memory of it all is recorded somewhere in the invisible, when we are in public we would never dare to do many things that would ashamed us, but the fact is, the creator omnipresence should be a deterrent for us to behave at all times as if we were in public, it's a silence spectator taking account of all our actions thoughts and feelings. This is very comforting, as we know it is all in our best interest, all of it has a reason, whether we understand it or not. I'm sure our creator wants everyone to know he is there with you, all the time, everywhere, he wants every human to grow to its fullest potential, we are the only ones in nature that settle for a lot less than we could, we must practice faith, trusting we have a purpose to pursue, our options are unlimited but, we choose a path and settle, or somebody else chooses the path for us and we settle, or circumstances choose what we do and where we going, and then we settle, it is so easy to just carry on, in the everyday routine and after a while, we realize this is not what I want or this is not where I want to stay, but we do little or nothing to change, it doesn't even take a lot of effort to do a small change that could potentially direct our direction to our dreams. Like if you don't brush your teeth every day, something small that only takes three minutes after a few months you will know and people around you would notice as well, if the book you been neglecting, you read it for ten minutes a day chances are you would finish one day and the sense of satisfaction, would increase your desire to go for another when you come from work eat and then after an hour or so you decide to jump on your car and go to the gym and jog or just do it around the block, instead of watching that program on television, even if you just do it a couple of times a week after a while you would start enjoying, and the sense of accomplishment is priceless, but most importantly the way your body changes and the way you look, exercise is the real fountain of youth, if instead of just letting the hours go by after work we start taking adult classes you just don't know what kind of opportunities might open, every small thing we do is important and every small thing we neglect can also rip our dreams slowly, Our time the most precious commodity always taken for granted like if we have an unlimited resource, but sadly is draining away the same way we drain a full tank of gas as we speed, when we run out of time we just do, or when someone decides to cut our life short by some stupid decision in their life committing a crime or in an accident; this must be very true as we have freedom of will, our freedom allows us to do good and bad our choice, allows us to do the things we must do or neglect them when at the end of the day we learn that our sacrifices at everything we did, was all worth it, our discipline to do the small things, to later on do greater things, discipline weights very little after a while, regret weights so much in the heart we might probably break the scale once we get old and look back sad and helplessly saying what I could have done differently, too late.

Many years ago I experience something similar in the sense of been ready when opportunity comes as once I heard Oprah W. say, I don't believe in luck, luck is preparation meeting the opportunity, this phrase stuck with me ever since; I remember working at a factory, building windows, it was the same thing over and over, day in, day out for some years, but I decided to take afternoon classes of electricity, one day when I finish several courses and when I was in my last one I remember knocking doors to work in that technical field but not one would hired me because my lack of hands on experience, I was demoralized but one day when we were just about finishing some guys from a Union of Electrical workers came to invite knew apprentices, from that class nobody care as they all got something bad to say about Unions due to I guess word of mouth, I don't know, but I decided to go to their office and ever since then, my life and income change for good, we must never rely on other people's opinion of things and circumstances as we all are different and we poses different charisma drive and will, to do something just because someone or too many had trip over a rock on the path, does not necessarily mean we will trip, try and then you will know only then. Preparation, even if everything is against you, when there is not even the slight chance or crack in the door where you can come in, where others opinions would think you are crazy and a fool to prepare for something, not one, even yourself, believe it would come true, when everybody doubts, it would ever happen, you just go ahead and do it, just because you feel good, just because it gives you a sense of accomplishment, just do it for you and when the day the door slightly open, you know how to walk in and then everybody would call it luck, yes indeed very lucky.

To our creator everything is possible, our little human understanding can't even grasp one millimeter in the thousands of Kilometers of knowledge and wisdom of God, the technology and science we know is like a drop of water in the ocean of knowledge, this knowledge we so much lack of and need; each one of us has a path a direction to follow, you are in the right place with the right people, with the right circumstances, our principal learning has nothing to do with how intellectual you can be or how much you can accumulate, and how much you can build, this is a misconception, as all this things would pass and have not value to God, as if you are very intelligent and rich, or you can be rich and ignorant, or both, you would still feel empty, lonely, frustrated, lost and angry, because you are disconnected as a result of the dissociation from your spirit, you are failing the test of life, inside growing is the most essential and fundamental, to feel a perpetual sense of joy peace and hope, with a blessing feeling all day, if we only knew the reason we're here, our journey would be so much easy, but we are here as a blank piece of paper with some gifts and inclinations since we are born, I believe if we look back when we were kids we had inclinations and things that really caught our attention and things that we really enjoy, during our most naive and fresh days is where we have to look deep for our purpose, because when we find it, we could as well expand our spirituality as we would do things from the heart, you can easily feel when someone sing from the heart, the difference is always incredible it can definitely touch other people, the same way, when we do what we are born to do, we will do it from the heart and we could touch others and your spiritually is connected to the things you do, by virtue of perfection and beauty. God created work and we can praise God with our everyday journey at work, when we do it from the heart if you have ever been in a hospital and a nurse helps you with genuine love and you get a sense of your mom or your Granma is helping you, you can easily identify who does it, as a vocation and who does it as a profession, as when we find our purpose, our heart leads the way. This is how our creator made things possible as a society we all complement each other to make one, we are all part of the orchestra and we need everyone's talent to sound amazingly beautiful.

> And if the ear should say, "Because I am not an eye, I do not belong to the body," that would not make it any less a part of the body. If the whole body were an eye, where would the sense of hearing be? If the whole body were an ear, where would the sense of smell be?
> 1 Corinthians 12:16-17

We all need each other; we just need to find our natural purpose to become the best ear, the best nose, and the best mouth, to benefit with our talents the world and this way to be of good service to others and the Lord.

To avoid the dissociation from the spirit; our Dec intoxication from all our everyday distractions has to be a discipline to impose, silence is the ideal but classical music would also help to get some calm and stress levels down, listen in silence without wondering in your always intruding and loud worries, listen if the spirit is trying to speak to you in the form of a thought unexpected as if it came from nowhere; but you must be careful for if you have old anger with someone or something, or if you are insecure as a result of jealousy, or if you have something bad you been carrying for many years or any weakness that you been carrying and struggling over a long time as a result of a corrupt life, be careful of the voices you might hear they might take you to a deeper sorrow, in those instances reading the word of God and prayer is the healer, before you find the silence, you must forgive, you must forget, you must let go, as all these feelings just hurt one person, you.

We should all pursuit greatness; greatness has nothing to do with money or possessions, physical beauty, ranks or power, greatness is a humble spirit, peaceful, and full of unconditional love, meek, without judging as judging would be our creator role to do, the invisible link to our creator wisdom is true greatness. This should be all of our ultimate goals, but the world has a different idea of greatness, how much you have,

Is how much you are worth, and all of us are buying this mistaken idea. As we tend to glorify those who had achieved large quantities of wealth.

Of all the virtues of the Universe Love is the most powerful force, is the bond of the Universe, if we practice love to all the people surrounding us at all times and everywhere we go, we start having good thoughts and sending blessings, praying for their wellbeing, we are getting close to reaching that which was our original design, we are getting close to reach and feel the power of the infinite intelligence working within you, hence we would be calm, we would walk at peace and people would intercept our thoughts.

And for the many mistakes and ignorance we walked in our past we most try to forgive ourselves for all those mistakes, we must pray for forgiveness, we made mistakes, we are here to learn, to take challenges, to grow and to have the inalienable right to be wrong, until we find the truth, and the truth is the word of God, the spiritual growth is full of challenges, and we only find it by choice and free will, this is perhaps our creator's plan, to grow through error and trial, he love us in a way not human could ever experience or understand for as many times as we err, he is extremely merciful, as he knows our entire life is to him like a drop of water in the ocean of eternity, his arms are wide open, we are free to do as we wish and every cause would have a consequence; for as you do, you would be, a life full of bitter, sadness, anger, worry and evil thoughts, or a life full of joy, peace and good thoughts, is either, or perhaps like in my case you have experienced many years of ignorance and now appreciate the priceless benefits of the other and much better life trying to do the right thing at all moments is not easy but is what all of us should strive for. If I could only describe lightly our Father's love for us, you will know why your mistakes are forgiven seventy times seven, if you have infant kids you love them, no matter what, even when they are sleeping you rejoice by just looking at them, and when they make mistakes, in your wisdom you know they don't have your knowledge and understanding and you just try to always teach them but your love for them is fuel to your spirit and when they look for you, hug you and kiss you, our heart is pure joy and whatever they do is clumsy and no matter how hard you try to teach them, there are many things they just would never be able to understand but is ok because they have you and when they call, you run to them because your love is connected to them even if they don't understand how much you love them.

We have the same seed, the same mold from the creation that makes us so much alike we might be different on the outside but all the same on the inside, if you smile at someone, that person would lower the invisible shield we use with strangers, when we look at someone with anger or talk harsh words, that person, if their spiritual growth is low, would, in turn, reciprocate the same attitude, but if the spiritual growth is higher they already forgive you, but it hurts, and if someone approaches you with a bad attitude you would behave according to your spiritual growth, either we use our primitive instinct or we just stay calm and move on, it is all the golden rule! "Do as to others, as you would want others, do unto you" How much we forget this on our day by day existence, is hard not to get emotional with many situations but to some degree all our learning has to direct our reaction to others, our reaction has to be, always a little better than yesterday.

If we could only feel like a big family, where we care for each other within our means, how much different this big home we call earth would be? We tend to think we are better; we tend to think we are smarter; we tend to think we know it all, and all of it is ok, it was a nugget of self-steam that was planted on purpose in our mind to survive and raise our heads, which would allow us to strive for something better, but that was just a small nugget of self-steam, but in fact, each one of us is unique, but we are all the same.

We understand this in the natural world, we know there are thousands of trees but it is a tree, some of them give lots of fruit, but in general, they are serving as filters for us to have clean oxygen, without mentioning the infinite uses they all have in our lives, we see many races of dogs, but it is a dog; too many of us tend to forget all humanity is the same, we have the same feelings the same needs, the same frustrations, but many different languages, traditions, color, culture, if we could only understand our neighbor, our friends, our coworkers, and strangers they are all like you and me, not different, we all need love, understanding, tolerance, respect, and many needs that help us go through our already hard lives.

We are not that different, just different circumstances when growing up, different weather, different language, but our core is the same, our continents divide us, our cultures divide us, our borders divide us some more and then our mind divide us a lot more, our Lord never promoted division, is our selfish nature who loves and nurture division.

This is one of the many purposes of writing this book, if we could just get the realization, like a fresh spring morning what we are, just one humanity striving for survival and looking for the same goal from infinite perspectives.

> Who can speak and have it happen if the Lord has not decreed it? Is it not from the mouth of the Most High that both calamities and good things come? Why should the living complain when punished for their sins?
> Lamentations 37-39

THE PURPOSE

> As he went along, he saw a men blind from birth. His disciples ask him, "Rabbi who sinned, this man or his parents, that he was born blind?" "Neither this man nor his parents sinned," said Jesus, "but this happens so the works of God might be displayed in him. John 9:1-4

Jesus cured this man of his blindness, perhaps the biggest purpose of this man in his life was the day Jesus was going to meet him, and open his eyes, so the world would always remember the power of Jesus when he walked among people. The meaning of his words goes beyond our reasoning, this man was born blind just to prove the works of God to generations of thousands of people in the future; his biggest purpose was probably achieved that day.

Just like that blind man, every one of us has a purpose, it may be something we may not even possibly imagine, our purpose might be to save someone life, to guide someone at a crucial moment, to teach others patience by all our wrong doing, to teach others tolerance for all our ignorance, teach others to love if we were born in any special way, to change others, to help others, and just like Judah betrayed Jesus misguided by satan, his role in this world was a lesson for us and to complete the mission of Jesus, there might be people whose mission might not be normal in any way of reasoning, but it is a purpose many times not understood and because not a single leaf falls from the tree without Gods approval, there are works of God that are beyond our understanding, the creator omnipotent and omnipresent only allows evil to do some work, but only what the creator allows it to; not more, as the power of the creator is unlimited even evil serve him, acknowledging or not.

We find our purpose as we walk the path that was traced for us, there would be signs, things, circumstances, tragedies, and times of trial, things unforeseen, by people who cross our paths come into our lives and change our world, usually, our heart leads the way, intuition, and places, we should never stop asking for guidance in prayer to find our purpose.

We have the freedom of thoughts, free will, to go where we want to and follow a path that would ultimately determine our present and future, but the result would be in direct proportion with our personal development.

If we close our eyes in prayer and silence, in those moments of loneliness, in those quiet moments, if we communicate our ideas, dreams, hopes, wishes, and troubles, either by voice or just thoughts, and we communicate our Lord everything as if we were talking to an old wise friend, and you don't doubt at any moment he is not listening, even when we think we are in the worst position any human can be, he is always there, our prayer would get the attention according to our faith and purpose. Jesus prayed before his big ordeal, but God knew his ordeal was the best way to send his message to the world and the best way to defeat the enemy, God was silent; everyone has a purpose and is always spiritual, not as we tend to think.

Our objective in life has always a good purpose, not to destroy, not to separate, and not to walk recklessly without direction; our purpose has a meaning, for us, for others, to better everything around, when good seed is planted good fruit comes out, is in our advantage to better our ways to future generations, and to have a life full of blessings, a heart full of joy and the peace that only comes with a good conscious, we may take the easy paths but slowly every part of us will become corrupt, slowly like a bad decease would start changing all of the good qualities we bring when we are born, we might change and adjust to the realities of our everyday life and grow in a fake perception of right and wrong slowly we will crawl like a slug, living a trail behind everywhere we go and that trail is all the dirt we emanate as a result of the paths we choose to take and the thoughts we think, our most closed relatives and friends would get hurt with our trail of pain and sorrow, we might even grow bigger and transfer this pain to much more people or we can be like a butterfly with a complete transformation once we start eating the right food for our mind and become even better of what we ever could, and there is always room to be better because only when we find higher levels of maturity we might be able to find the wisdom to realize the greatest purpose in life is to glorify and to love God with the things we do every day, with our mind and with love.

Eighty years of life is the average of the majority of us, is not that much time at all, we need to use the economy of our entire life wisely and be conscious, every minute is a chance to glorify and to love but if we are infected with so much arrogance we will find instead fault constantly in others making us very edgy and without noticing we would find ourselves fighting and getting angry at others how do I know because I lived this way for so long and I know this attitude is repulsive to our Lord, but if instead, we find some equilibrium, to understand, for the sake of peace; I found many times in my life, peaceful people, this kind of person hardly ever gets in any conflict, and people who have a bad attitude for life and others is always in trouble and getting angry constantly and maybe they may even walk through the same circumstances and get different results, what is the food we use for our mind and our spirit? We can't give what we don't have, a poison plant fruit is poisonous, only when we fuel the fire of rage it keeps growing when we cool it down it diminishes but if we don't have a peaceful heart we are only pleasing the enemy, perhaps we ignore Jesus is the prince of peace, sometimes we don't even have to do great things to glorify God just change the tune but if we keep feeding our mind and spirit with all the noise this world offers, how can we react differently? Impossible, this world demands us to be tough, is only when we start directing our attention to the gospels we grow the seed of peace, and when we follow our libidine without regard just to please the flesh, we deviate more and more, is not our purpose in life, it is for something more meaningful more deep more strong is for love, because is in there where we are in the same dimension with our creator, there are many ways to live a life, there are many roads all of us will take but make no mistake, no matter where we go, and how far we think we reach if we don't glorify God with our life, everything we have accomplished is dust and everything we have done is trash, even if to the eyes of the whole world you have accomplished a lot. And if we are touched by the mercy of God and change and begin to bear fruit, all the mistakes we made, would help us, help others not to follow the same path, to correct the wrong we did, and help those who are getting infected with all those deceases that are killing families, friends, mothers, fathers, sisters, brothers, and our entire society, we are all in needs of love, this huge gift we lack so much nowadays, we live in a society where we see everyone as a potential enemy, we need so much love to cure all the souls that are falling in the dark abysm.

FORGIVE

Everyone has the power to forgive just like Jesus at the last moments of his life, asked the father to forgive them, even after he was mocked, scorned and tortured; he was treated like a criminal when he had the most impeccable behavior.

> "Father, forgive them, for they do not know what
> they do"
> Luke 23:34

There is a power you acquire when you forgive, there is a weight you release when you forgive, your resentment and pain would no longer be yours, and you would feel lighter and the love of God would be there to comfort you and give you strength.

As much as we think we know and think we have control of things, all our actions when we carry the burden of pain would more likely bring more and more pain in a chain of events that if we follow our instincts, we would ultimately, suffer and regret.

While we are alive, we would experience pain, doubt, sorrow, loneliness, sadness and sometimes you would feel like your existence is meaningless and without a purpose at times, but that is part of the always learning process every one of us has to go through, is part of our spiritual education, we get what we need, not what we want at the moment we need it. And many times our Lord uses other people to help us grow; the ones who cause so much pain, tears, and sorrow are in many ways our teachers. Jesus taught us to pray without ceasing, and especially during those difficult and hard moments is imperative, as this would make us strong and resilient. Not one said it was easy but it's necessary, prayer helps us get through with strength that comes from above and within.

If I'm helping my kid ride his bike and the frustration and pain make him kick the bike and throw it away, I will not ride the bike with him after his frustration, unless I feel he needs that for a minute to regain strength and try again, I don't believe is any different from our Father, our prayers help regain hope to keep on going, to start fresh. We will not go on in life without troubles or challenges, as one of the main goals of life is for new and never-ending experiences.

I remember throughout the majority of my entire life I had strong feelings about my father who I never meet in my life, he left, many times for the lack of love or understanding couples break apart, but the father is always there but in my case I never knew what it was like to have a father, many times my grandfather was what I remember most about a father figure, but what tear me in pieces was the fact he never once came back to his kids, not for birthdays, not for Christmas not never, my mother struggle to survived and provide, as I was growing up my pain and resentment remain, but when this feeling really stroke my heart was when I had kids as I consider them such a blessing, I realize if I had to leave for any reason my heart would tear in pieces, during that time of this realization I cried like I never cried before and some of the pain and resentment wash away, but much more still remain until in my late thirties I decided to let go and forgive him, it was a decision I made that would only help me, as with any other resentments it only hurts and damages the one who carries all the burden of pain, to the point of many times generating diseases and a bitter and sour heart, the burden in my heart was heavy, I didn't want to carry it any more, it was killing me inside out, I just realize it was time to let go. Even with all the negative feelings I had, I said I forgive you, I forgive you and I bless you, I cried and I let go, those negative feelings slowly started to disappear off my heart, nowadays I pray for him often as he didn't know any better; ignorance is for the majority of man the worst enemy, we all make mistakes, I pray from my heart for him and it feels good, especially when he probably went on happy with his life and meantime this pain was in my heart, it wasn't worth it, late in my forties I meet him, shook his hand and talked it was just a friendly encounter; just like this example all of us might have strong feelings we need to get rid of, it is the only way out.

"But if you do not forgive people their offenses, your
Father will not forgive your offenses."
Matthew 6:15

I wish there was a recipe for forgiveness, is not easy at all, but is always better to empty the load with lots of tears or let the pain become a monster and transform our life into a living nightmare for all the ones we love around us.

But now on these days, it is a lot more difficult to forgive offenses daily, as if someone treated us and offensively talk to us, our natural response is to get angry and reciprocate, but if we want the perfection our Lord is looking for, we must stop, respond nicely and ignore, it feels good to keep your inner peace intact, same procedure bless them, a small prayer for them and go on, I know from personal experience is not easy but if we want to move up in the ladder to a true love we can't look back and be the same we always been, as every day is a new battle where at the end of the day we must be victorious.

If for every resentment we get through in our life, we acquire rock and place it on a bag and carry it everywhere we go, it would eventually be so heavy we would be hurt, we would be cranky, angry, and ready to blow up, but most times sad and empty, this is true as our heart is where we keep these rocks and as we go on in life they weight more and more every day, and the worst part about it, is the fact the people who harm us, are probably fine, we can't let the actions of others determine our future forever, we have to let go and live our life at peace; there is just no other way. And if you think revenge is the way, jails, cemeteries, and hospitals are the dwells of many who chose that option.

Do not take revenge, my dear friends, but leave room
for God's wrath, for it is written: "It is mine to avenge; I
will repay," says the Lord. On the contrary:

"If your enemy is hungry, feed him; if he is thirsty, give him something to drink. In doing this, you will heap burning coals on his head. "Do not be overcome by evil, but overcome evil with good. Romans 12:19-20

If just by remembering the offence we could heal and slowly recover then it will be worth, keeping it in the memory and heart, but remembering the offence in many circumstances causes all kinds of anger issues and in many others just pain, why do we play the picture over and over, many times for years, if only by remembering we could fix anything, but unfortunately we can't, the only thing we accomplish is becoming bitter and bitter every day, but if you are strong enough to make the decision and let go, you won't ever forget the offence but you will let go and slowly you will forgive, all of us are learning, all of us grow with so many difficulties and hurdles and the majority of times the offender acted for pure ignorance and lack of love, spiritually poor just like all of us who are surfing the waves of life, I dare to say all of us have been offenders too at one point in our lives, we acted in complete ignorance because it takes a whole life to learn, we were created but not a final product yet, we are constantly been created, make the decision to let go and try not to play the movie of the offence ever again, there is nothing you can change except, perhaps you might get sick physically and spiritually, you are much better than the offender and if you are reading this is because your spirit is hungry, keep on feeding it with healthy words and never stop praying.

THE TRACKS

When two men are together in a dark cave but one man is blind, while they are in the dark, both are in the same condition, when the light comes on, the men who can see has an advantage over the blind and knows where he is going, therefor when a man acknowledge Jesus and his word in his heart, sees where he is going and how to get there, the unbeliever chooses ignorance and darkness.

With sadness today I read an article about how millennials are abandoning religion and church due to the amount of wrongdoing they see others do while they are in religion, they are judging the teachings of the master due to a lot of bad students and some bad teachers, while is true many people in religion might have a double life and probably do many mistakes regularly does this mean the teaching of the master is wrong and fake? Does this mean we have to walk away from class because every other student is messing up and abandoning our careers? Our most important one we would be uneducated in matters of spirit where we potentially would be at the mercy of the enemy of the spirit, the only one that hates everything about Jesus and hates every human because when we are baptized we become sons and daughters of our Lord. While is true the majority of people at church had trouble past and even if everything in their life appears to be normal, they have much more troubles than many think, why? because the church is a hospital of the sick where all of us who once were ill in the spirit are still healing but doesn't necessarily mean we already heal, is a process that requires a whole life, many inside, indeed tend to judge more because many of us think, because we attend church we try to be good and help, we already won a ticket to heaven but is a gathering of many ill people on many levels spiritually, we are many broken pieces trying to follow the perfection of Jesus, making mistakes every day but if you don't attend a class where would you learn? If you don't go to a hospital, how would you heal? Yes they are many bad students but we all have a judge waiting at the door for when we pass on the afterlife, even if the law of the men never reaches you for the wrongdoing in this life, at the moment we pass our judge is waiting…

> And just as it is appointed for man to die once, and
> after that comes judgment, Hebrews 9:27

The enemy hates the fact he would never be a son of the Lord, we have the privilege if we choose to, and people without the knowledge of the truth from the teachings of the master, become easy targets, the more and more people walk away from Jesus the more this world would be at the mercy of the enemy and the day will come when acknowledging or by ignorance become instruments of Satan and will attack and be against the teachings of the master Jesus and his followers, judging them as fanatics but this has happened trough history since the radical teaching of Jesus, not one should be afraid in fact not one who follows Jesus should be intimidated but we should feel sad for all those who by choice turn their back on Jesus just because the works of the enemy have infiltrated the classroom to deceive those who are outside; If our Lord could show them the truth they would run to church and start learning everything about God, but this unfortunate times are here to stay and grow bigger and stronger as the evil is taking more and more over the whole world injecting a dose of relativism. Jesus came to the world to tell us all the secrets that were hidden for generations before he came, is up to us to believe, during his time many saw his works and yet didn't believe, what we can expect these days when many think all of it, is just blurry history, and perhaps a God so far in the distance, I wish and pray many could come back and believe as it hurts to see even after all the sacrifice Jesus endure many would still reject his mercy, forgiveness, and love.

Our conscious becomes anesthetized when we abandon the church and

Jesus, as there is not one to tell us, right and wrong; we don't want to hear what our "self-stubborn, intellectual and analytic mind can't understand" the message written in the scripture, the truth, our slumber self would allow everything our imagination or whatever we want to do and think, if it is wrong we would find an intellectual and social way to approve it, just to peace our sleepy conscious that way, we can continue doing whatever we want and more, we get a distorted peace of mind, but the reality is that we slowly open many obscure doors that we can't close, we fail to clearly understand what is wrong and what is right as we acquired a wrong sense of right, as the teachings of Jesus and the church are like the tracks of a train, there is only one way for the train not to derail is to keep running on those tracks, the teachings of Jesus were written for all of us to keep on those tracks and stay until the last day, there is only one way to keep moving on, Jesus is the way, we cannot fool ourselves thinking we can go on with just our strength we just don't have it, even if for many years we go on like nothing is wrong, slowly we become affected by our disguised sin, there are times in everyone life where the master call us, this might be by another person that impact us and who's wording almost wake our conscious up, there might be something we read, something we hear somewhere, or when tragedy strikes to show us we are not gods who even after we accomplish so much and we have done so many successful things, we are nothing, we have no power of our own and everything we have received was not because our self-fight, it was given to us even if we can't accept this fact.

Tragedy strikes as a way to humble a proud spirit sometimes the tough need a tighter grip to realize who we are, as this is mercy from the creator before we face the judge, but even after this so many calls, many people don't recognize the call from above for their good and sake.

We really cannot do anything without the help from above, we might be deceived to think otherwise but we cannot, yes this is a mystery as God is full of mysteries, perhaps for many of us, it would be too late the day we realize this truth maybe the day we are on our judgment, how terrible this certainty would be, we need to always pray for the non-believers.

It is a fearful thing to fall into the hands of the living
God. Hebrews 10:31

> *For God so loved the world, that he gave his only Son, that whomever believes in him should not perish but have eternal life. John 3:16*

Why is so difficult to believe these days? Why was so difficult to believe back when Jesus was alive? Why has been so difficult through all times to accept his message? When he was alive there was too much pride and envy, too much jealousy of the many followers he had, jealousy of the wisdom he possessed, he did not respect the Saturday in their eyes and because he call himself the Son of God, they thought they knew who his father was, they thought Joseph was his real father, they didn't understand the deep mystery of his incarnation, God works are hidden and this is a mystery as well, during that time they use their intelligence to deduce he was just the son of Joseph, but to the followers, they didn't understand but they saw all his works and miracles and they believe his words and wisdom they use their heart and spirit not their minds even when most of the messages were hidden inside parables, they were in the dark, they fell in love with a man whose presence illuminated the hearts of the humble.

Of all the secrets in the whole world the most beautiful secret is the life and works of Jesus; all of those who look for riches dig them in the scripture and you would find the most precious treasure, all of those looking for fame look in to the scripture and you would find joy in the most famous person in history, all of those looking for truth love, for real love, dig in the scripture to find a unconditional love, a love who would never betray you, a love who would never let you down, a love you would never find on any existing human, as our love in relations is defective, perhaps we would never love the way we are meant to, while we live here, if you looking for peace, if you looking to be comforted as the burden you carry is too much to bear, find the comfort in the scripture as the window in to the mind of our creator help us fill all our needs and our wildest dreams, is a secret open to all of us, a secret that truly lift the spirit, a secret that really works a secret told for all men to find salvation, a secret who's voice was silence on a cross two thousand years ago but still echoing through his disciples year after year century after century to restore hope and to join the kingdom of the light.

Let us continue to hold firmly to the hope that we confess without wavering, for the one who made the promise is faithful. Hebrews 10:23

Ultimately we are just like children always in need of learning and for this reason, so many teachers take advantage, so many people believe many things and everything turns out so confusing and nothing is so bad, with this supermarket of so many things to believe, many of them seem deep, relaxing, exotic and attractive, the stars, the planets, the stones, the antique practices of the Mayans, mother earth, the exercise and position of our bodies to find the inner self, the objects that supposedly bring luck, or so many other inputs from antique pagan cultures, they might feel like something we could practice and believe with no harm, but is harmful, as they slowly start making us lose perception of the only truth, is like putting cheese with little poison, the same way we have tried to kill mice, fading the truth and distorting it, this goes to many wrongful interpretations of the scripture from wrong leading pastors too, if we ever hear the truth from the gospels, but if we haven't we simply follow because it makes me feel nice. With so many different things to believe not wonder so much confusion, especially our younger generations every day more and more join the files of the ones who chose a little of everything some meditation from Asian cultures, some objects for luck, a little from here and there or nothing at all, we might get sick and confuse and at the end never really find what we want to accomplish, to find the inner peace, some look for the magic in lucky objects, those are always empty promises not different from those old pagan cultures that had always believe so many and so diverse lies. The only winner here is the enemy of our souls because with so much confusion and the lack of knowledge mistakes are inevitable the sense of emptiness, loneliness, and the lack of fear to do evil. We, on the other hand, have the reassurance of the truth when our savior was resurrected; he prove the truth of his message when he resurrected, and as the scripture said the fear of God is the beginning of wisdom just like a well-behaved child fears his father, this is where we have to be careful, into what we believe and what we listen to, so many of us fall into traps, of the new age, Christianity is a lifestyle that gives fruit in the soul in the spirit and our everyday actions, we need to be like children to be open to learning, to love, but children who know who their father is and never go with an estranger, unlike infants who can be taken and be feed by any mothers milk and learn anybody's teaching, and be carried by anybody's arms.

MY OWN QUESTIONS

There is a point In your life you need some answers, you become like a four year old kid at the age of "whys," and perhaps if you really want answers you would probably start searching, reading, meditating, and wondering where is the answer, and maybe you will end up with more questions, the truth is that you are searching for yourself, to find the meaning of your life, it is the internal clicking of the clock, letting you know, you must hurry to find the true wisdom you came to this world to acquire, your spirit wants to bring you back to your tracks, the real purpose, to be a better you in all aspects of your life, and to find the love; the love for yourself, love for your life because it is unique, love for the people you share this journey with, and the passengers who come and go, understanding that everything is temporary all circumstances change, especially if they are harsh, because a better you will eventually emerge, out of bad circumstances we grow, when it rains the plants the flowers and trees grow and everything seem to be alive after a rain, when it rains in our life we also grow, find love for the place you live, love for all the creatures on this planet and beyond specially your own kind, even if you don't agree with their thinking, when we are born we all come in the same way and start somehow with our own blank sheet of paper, and when we go, either we leave a legacy or we just die with a name and the half a million dollars or more in the products we consumed in our entire life, one thing is for certain, we can just pass by, without ever realizing the need to learn a new philosophy of life, one that would enrich our life and the life of others. One that would make our life more enjoyable and peaceful with any resource we may have at any period of our life, and in the process enrich others with everything we have to give

Why?

When we are kids our parents and teachers either they limit our capacity or expanded it, by example and by the rules and words they impose in our early life, if we grow with limited believes and we don't change our philosophy we could stand still and watch others pass by getting ahead in life; is our limited believes we impose in our mind, if someone excel in life we tend to think they are smart and they are lucky, but the truth with few exceptions is that they have persistence and discipline while the majority of us lived our lives with self-impose limitations.

After a hard working day we tend to feel worn out our stress and anxiety levels are at its peak, and we seem to think we are on a hamster wheel just getting nowhere and you ask, is this all there is for me? How can we really make a change even if all odds are against, the answer to all our troubles, not matter your circumstances, your pain, your attitude, your health, you must always feed your mind, nourish your mind like you would a beautiful plant, but unfortunately it is one of the most neglected things we do, because when we let our surroundings and environment feed our small and powerful asset we end up the way we don't want to, at the place we don't want to, with the circumstances we don't want to, we curse the result but neglect the cause.

This is a secret but is not a secret at all, feed your mind, whatever your definition of success might be your mind is the pilot designer architect, and engineer, involuntarily or voluntarily of our present reality, a new you will emerge even if you don't see it, in the physical now, in your environment and surroundings, change your mind and everything would happen accordingly beautiful things would manifest, people around would have a better attitude, better things would start happening. There is beauty everywhere, look for it, "find the greatness in you," there is a lot of more we can give, there is a lot more we could do for others and this beautiful home we call earth, greatness has nothing to do with money, possessions, ranks or power, greatness is love, humility, kindness, forgiveness, respect for that which you didn't create, greatness is the invisible link to our creator wisdom, that where infinite intelligence reaches to all existence to all matters, forms and existence, where all your senses feel the energy and feed from it. The worst thing that can happen to a human mind is to be wasted, so vast and so deep like an ocean is the unexplored human mind if each of us can contribute putting our seed in society, to be better, to grow, to enhance our living we would have not limited in what we could do and as far as we can go just like it has happened in the past two centuries, the realization of many that our potential is almost limitless, but as with any learning the spirit has to be on top of the list because it transcends.

What is behind everything we do? Of all the powers of the Universe love is the most powerful force, the unconditional love to all and everything, start having good thoughts toward all, bless everything, the power of your blessing gives you energy as any blessing you give away would come back to you, as we do this we are getting close to reach and feel the power of the good God working within us, hence we would be calm, we would walk at peace, and forgive yourself for all your pass mistakes and ignorance as you didn't know any better, we walked a path of ignorance, we slowly left the dark behind, you are a new person, you are not what you used to be maybe ten, or fifteen or twenty years ago, or perhaps something happens in your life that you are not what you used to be just a year ago, yes we can change and this is a gift, as no other creature on this planet can choose to change as we do when we change we start getting more of the invisible force that unites the whole universe, love.

Is it possible to abandon all our weaknesses and bad habits behind? It's not just possible is a fact, is a decision with discipline, true knowledge is a process, you can't change a lifetime of bad habits and weaknesses in ten days or just one book, one seminar is a slow process of learning, the majority of animals in the world only required limited time before they go on their own, unlike humans, where the process takes about twenty years just to be somehow independent. Our brain is so complex we need time to develop properly. It is a slow process, to a definite change but is well worth it, for the individual who is willing to have a better life, a bad habit or an addiction, with the right discipline and self-inducing knowledge it might take just a year or a couple, but complex and deep-rooted addictions or psychological problems may require a long time, to abandon one bad habit that we might think is impossible to eradicate from our life, any bad habit is a mental weakness and almost certainly, that weakness is just one of many other corrupt habits in one's self, as if I smoke, is not just the cigarette, chances are, there may be some other weakness behind the cigarette and behind this one, there may be some other, because whatever bad habit you allow to be your master, you will always be a slave and thus a deep mental weakness. And mental weakness is an open door to many other corruptions. And one bad habit maybe just one brick of our corrupted castle.

If it's possible to change, then how to do it? I can personally assure you is possible as I was as corrupted in the spirit as a person can get, I'm not what I was some years ago, and I'm blessed to have overcome those things that slave me for all my life, and I just would never think, it would be possible to eradicate them forever, for example, I had a short spark I could easily lose my temper, and prompt to be violent, I was very fast to criticize, I was proud, arrogant, and I could go on, I smoke for a few years, my mind was corrupted up until my forties, when I started feeding my mind. Quitting smoking was extremely difficult but I force myself to do it after I join a gym, but smelling the cigarette would make me just crave for one more all the time, but I fought that craving with exercise until one day just went away, not without been tempted for several times as with any weakness once you let it go and you think you are strong, there would be tempting times the moment you are more vulnerable, I don't know who set this arrangement but if you ever have a weakness and you quit, just be prepared for the test, when you least expected, the enemy wants to keep you slave, free yourself it's not just possible is necessary you owe it to your love ones, you owe to yourself, things and circumstances around you would get better in every way, our mind can be molded, and our body would just follow because a realization to get fit would come naturally, if we keep active, doing productive things and then just keep the momentum going, as we have to remember our muscles would get weak if we don't exercise them; do you ever have the feeling of been so much more tired after you rest for a long weekend or just rest for a long time and when is time to go back to your duties you just feel extremely tired, it seem as the only rest the majority of people really need is just one night sleep, I'm not Doctor but I believe a lot of injuries when we are mature are mostly due to our weak back muscles, our weak muscles in general, I personally got a lot of shoulder and back pains heal with moderated exercise not pain killers. Or when you spend a lot of time searching improper stuff on the internet and perhaps you think is normal as the media bombard us everywhere with all kinds of subliminal messages and it gets inside your mind as "normal," I got news for you, it is not, it distorts your mind and promotes promiscuity, and if you think you have an addiction, a weakness, a corruption, it's in your best interest to start eradicating this evil from your life, as if you think that when you walk inside your house all this evil stays outside waiting for you to come back outside you are wrong, you bring this evil to every member in your family who share the same roof with you, those who are receptive to your bag of corruptions could as well, may become contaminated, I remember how one day after a rage of bad temper my little daughter had her fists tight and her eyes were full of anger looking at me, because every little thing would make me mad and I wanted my little one to behave like an adult, that was my harvest.

All you have to do is become addicted to things that would make you a better person, join a gym, find a group that offers support, find a church, read-only material that would help you and bring the best of you, when on the internet find knowledge and entertainment things that would inspire you and make you smile, things that teach you and make you a better person, if you like movies also try not to see too many things that would hurt you, and bring your emotions to a negative state and also brings your weakness afloat, engage in any activity that could keep your mind off your weakness, think about Jesus or your love ones when in temptation.

But if you want to be strong memorize bible verses and repeat them when you feel weak, because the word of God is powerful and destroys everything that has its source in the darkness and comes as a weapon to overcome your weak will.

When an angry person comes your way looking to bring the worst in you, stay calm refrain your ego from trying to win an argument or show up, your ego might be telling you how tough you are, and you should not take it if you give in, you just let the other person control you, and not the other way around, you have control, you can control the situation, this is a real character, listen to the little voice inside telling you to stay calm, get disconnected from the moment and pray, it works wonders, pray while the other person argues so you don't listen remain in control you are the boss inside your mind. Many don't realize evil can transmit thoughts into people how do we know that? Remember when Jesus told Peter to stand back satan because you don't think like God, this verse in the bible gives us a clever clue, why? Because evil cannot support the word of God therefor if you fight with the word of God in the form of mental quotes you memorize he would flee right away.

Why so much pain and suffering? If we could reduce the answer to this question I would say ego, ambition, and ignorance.

Ignorance because at many times in our life or the life's of other people who come across our paths, our decisions are based on what we know during that time and not true wisdom, and the decisions others take also affect our existence for the same reason "ignorance", we can't blame ourselves, we can't blame others, when all of us, only had a limited vision and very little knowledge when we did what we did. Can we excuse our actions and the actions of others? We can't do that, wrong is wrong whether we knew it or not, during that time we were doing it, but the day we recognize our wrongdoing and stop doing it, we must forgive our past and move on because if you torture yourself this would bring anxiety, depression, sadness.

Ambition because a great share of wars, destruction, pain, and sorrow was in great part for the immeasurable ambition of the humans, as the human ambition is like a black and dark hole, that can't be filled, for the sake of ambition so much has been destroyed and sacrifice and lives lost, ambition lives in the heart of all man and it has to be controlled and restricted if we don't we will suffer twice one because you can't ever fill a man's heart and the other because in the search to fulfill our ambition we will harm us and others, Now there is a positive ambition, one the drives a person to succeed and bring the best in you and develop every aspect of your life and those you love.

Ego, this one, the monster of all evils, as this one does so much damage in our personal life and worldwide, so much pain, so many lives have been destroyed by ego, how many families separated by ego, how many enemies are created by ego, how many wars and thousands of people have been lost on the sake of someone ego, it may seem like is everywhere and always showing his shiny and evil smile, it feeds with everything we are, and is never satisfied, is the one that make us want to hurt others and lots of times the people we love the most, those are the ones who take straight punches from our ego, this monster is the one that, even when we know, we are all the same, ego make us think we are better because we are toll, because we are lean, because we are pretty, because we are stronger, because we are black, white, brown or blue, because I have material possessions others don't have, or my account is bigger and we feel we are so much better than others, but we can't be more far away from the real true, the way God see each and every one of us is so much different, he sees through the skin straight to the heart and weights each and every one of us by the way we really and truly are, he don't care about your looks and how strong or smart you are, he don't care how many possessions we think we own, because if we have it now it is only something we just borrow from the creator and he can claim it back, at any moment, we are so easily cheat with what we see, we judge with the eyes, but I'm sure you would agree with me, if we could be able to see the way God sees through our skin we would be so surprise to find and realize where true beauty and greatness really are; it may seem like since we are born this monster slowly stars growing and later on, in life is so hard to control, that is if we are humble enough to admit we have a great deal of this monster growing inside if not we will never know we have it and would never even try to suppress it.

How much do we feed it? Every time we have any sense of superiority for whatever the reason is, we are feeding it, every time we feel we don't need anybody, we are feeding it, every time we think we know the answer for everything we are feeding it, every time we feel powerful, we are feeding it, every time we lost touch with our so weak and fragile humanity we are feeding it, if you don't believe we are weak, go visit a hospital a place where our ego is brought back to the floor and step on, ego should be public enemy number one, but is the other way around, its constantly feed on, praise on, with the media and so many other forms of subliminal messages, it is probably impossible to eradicate our ego but we should have it under control, not allowing it to take charge of our everyday life, we have to remember to keep our feet on the ground and recognize our humanity, meaning that we are full of greatness and full of err, we were born to be imperfect but we were born to strive for better, even when is out of reach, every day is a new battle a new beginning a new challenge to keep away the one thing that does so much harm to us and the people who is orbiting around our life, keep ego out of our everyday life one day at time.

Nebuchadnezzar an ancient king of Babylon own a huge empire

during that time, he was a really powerful king like no other had ever been in history, but he was full of pride when he was told by Daniel about the meaning of a dream where he was the head of a statue a golden king of kings, instead of glorifying God for all he gave him, after this dream he created a statue of himself for everyone to bow, after that he saw a miracle with his own eyes when he burns three men for not bowing, and they survive with the hand of God, he didn't change much. But God is about to show him, and leave it as a testimony for all humanity to realize where everything comes from and who is in charge of our leaders and kings, pride is one of the things that our creator detest the most as the firstborn rebel angel harbor this seed and became full of it, we should be careful when we start to the harbor and feed this seed is the complete opposite of Jesus who despite having the condition of God, he was so humble, since the moment he was born as the conditions of his birth were so unfair, for someone who was king and someone who was coming to be a savior, but this is where our father hides the seed of perfection is the opposite of pride, humility is the most terrible weapon to hurt and destroy the devil, but this world is meant to and was built by men, to harbor pride; be careful when you see perfection in you.

From the book of Daniel:

The pride of Nebuchadnezzar was strong, and he didn't turn from his pride even after he was confronted by the power of God for a second time. This time it was Shadrach, Meshach, and Abednego who were Jews exiled from Judah that made an impression of their God onto Nebuchadnezzar. Nebuchadnezzar created a statue of himself made from pure gold and placed it on the plain of Dura for people to bow down and worship him there. Every time they play any instrument, those who would not bow down to the idol were cast into a great furnace. When the trumpets sounded, three men stood while the crowds of men all knelt to worship the king of Babylon. Those men were Shadrach, Meshach, and Abednego. For this reason, they were thrown into the fire, the king ordered the fire to be seven times hotter than normal, and the men that threw them in were killed because the furnace was so hot, but the three survived the furnace. After they came out of the fire, Nebuchadnezzar praised the God of heaven for saving them, but he was harbored pride in his heart. Shortly after, he boasted about his works: how he rules the kingdom and how he built up and fortified all of the cities in Babylon, on the same day he was having these thoughts he lost his kingdom.

After seeing the boastfulness of the king, God was set to destroy the pride of King Nebuchadnezzar. He sent his servant, Daniel, to tell Nebuchadnezzar that he would be driven out from society and that he would eat grass in the fields like the cattle for seven years. And so it was. King Nebuchadnezzar lost his speech and he became like a beast of the fields. Meanwhile, Daniel ruled the Babylonian Empire, and there was peace for seven years. When Nebuchadnezzar regained his sanity, he professed that God is the only living God, and that He is higher than any other, and that He builds up kingdoms by His own will.

If we could just think for a minute about where we going tomorrow, to the place where we don't need anything we think is valuable, to the where the only thing we take is what we are, don't let that ego steal great moments with your love ones, don't let that ego create problems and make you say or do things that would hurt others, don't let that ego hurt you accept the fact we age, we are just like a flowering cycle, we are a seed that grows and bloom then withers and dies, don't fight it, trying to glue the fallen petals, take aging with pride and dignity as a wither rose has its beauty, aging brings the one thing we lack most of our life, "wisdom."

Many times when our ego is so much inflated that blinds us, we don't realize we make everybody sick and the people around us try to keep a distance, and avoid confrontation as our head is hermetically closed to anything that contradicts what we believe or think, we are loud because we need the attention we feed on, we are so self-center, estrangers despise us when we raise our head and open our mouth but inside our stagnant intelligence we are great, sharp, smart, tough, but in reality, we are just fools.

When Jesus apostles, were arguing about who was greatest among them as their inevitable human behavior was taking …

> He sat down, called the twelve disciples over to him,
> and said, "Whoever wants to be first must take last place
> and be the servant of everyone else.
> Mark 9:35

In our everyday life, how agreeable is it when you meet someone humble whose charm is hard to resist, whose sincere smile and calm comments are like freshwater, open to suggestions, a quiet and easy-going personality? Those who are most humble and self-denying mirror a great deal, Jesus Christ.

How much I desire to be of this nature, we should all strive for this behavior, and how difficult is to overcome the big mountain of trash we have and is represented in the "I" the moment we bring "I am, I need, I have, is me," into anything is our ego calling, those who are full ego mirror a great deal the fallen angel, the enemy of all good.

I remember some years ago when I was on my job, I was an electrician apprentice I had a foreman not one really liked, his personality was arrogant, loud, offensive with his words and his way was the only right way, he enjoyed the argument, slave driver, despotic and self-center, many times I wonder who could live with someone like that, as he was married, that was a mystery to me, I hardly ever had any argument with him as I was a good worker, I always did what I was told on time, but many others had lots of problems with this guy, and not just electricians, many other guys working on other trades, as well, despise him, they had portable toilets for the construction and this guy name was all over written in those porta-toilets walls, with so much profanity, this would in turn cause this guy to lose his already lost nerve, and this would definitely be the cause for more trouble, or argument somewhere else, I used to wonder there must be a lot pressure in his shoulder to keep his image as a tough person, know- it all and self-confident guy, when people would get transfer to another job they were so happy, when I was transferred I always felt relieved too, even if I didn't have any problems with him, but just from hearing all the drama and the tension on the job was enough to bring the spirit down, as I work with him some times during those days, there was a lot energy wasted on the negative personality of this guy, and most times whomever he came in contact with, as many times his eyes would give you that mean look that he didn't have to say anything, why was so difficult, or perhaps impossible to be nice to others, I wonder if that ego was after all responsible for this unhealthy behavior, this toxic kind of personality is spotted at many places in our paths as we go on, in our journey, sometimes there is not reasoning on this subjects and they bring a lot of tension on the already hard as it is job, and many times the only thing we do is pray for this person and hoping sometime soon leave somewhere else, is hard not to be affected especially when this behavior is bully to others, and is worst if this person has some kind of authority is like giving a scorpion wings, is during those times and specially those times when we have to disconnect from where we are either we find a better place to work, we talk to the next level above this person, we ask for a transfer, because our sanity affects everyone at home, but if none of this is possible we need to reach out to God, pray and pray ask in a humble manner, no one comes to our lives without reason.

THE ENEMY

We can't recognize it, if we don't want to, we can't see it if we don't realize is there, we could live our entire life sharing every moment with our enemy, and we could never see it, other times our close family members or friends might not see it either, we know is there but we just can't fight it, we don't have the strength or the tools to fight it, and decide one day it's a permanent tenant in our life, we give in, other times we just too lazy to pick a fight and face it, or too scary and we just ignore it, or perhaps it gives us a small amount of joy and pleasure but a lifetime of guilt and pain. The enemy is within every person and nobody, but our own conscious can really know what it is, we must take a detail and deep introspection to find what or who the enemy is, we can't lie to our own selves, we can lie to others if you want to, but the things we are slaves of, the things we consider our weakness, the things we think we need in our life but in reality are just causing harm to us and others, the things we do or say to cause pain in others, in a mirror we see our face we see the physical form of our humanity, in the same way we must search deep inside and find who the enemy is within, all of us have our own personal enemy or enemies destroying our life, and the lives of our love ones and our community, this bad habits, behaviors or unconscious things we do that have become part of our personality and deep inside we know are causing harm, many times we acquire certain behaviors, we don't even know we have and became a toxic person, but if we look around and some of the people who we deal with, every day has a problem with us we should look deep inside, if John has a problem with Tom, and John has a problem with Peter and John has a problem with Mark, the problem is probably John and perhaps and most likely John doesn't even know, he is more likely very angry and frustrated with others, his nerves are to the edge; not knowing who the enemy is, it has become a heavy burden on his life, if we tend to have problems with almost everyone we have to look deep inside perhaps we use harsh words or are rude in our manners or authoritarian demeanor, many things we do or say are affecting others and thus affecting us; a kind, respectful and gentle person is hardly going to be finding problems with others, this is part of the self-retrospection, as many of the behaviors we have due to our past, have a negative effect on the personality we now have.

But if we don't know the enemy, we can't fight it, if we don't really know who we fighting with, we can't go to a battle if we don't know who the enemy is, we should really know if we really want to eradicate all evil from our life, if we happen to get a clue and just do small changes to improve, and not really get it off our heart and mind, we are just fooling ourselves as if we just cut the branches but leave those roots, it will one day slowly grow again, and if we feed it with the rain of our everyday toxic life, perhaps toxic friends, toxic habits and especially if we don't really know the power of the word of God or if we know it but is fading slowly, it may be only a matter of time before we come back to our old ways, we have to cut down to the root and remove it; every single bad habit or bad behavior had a beginning we did it one day out of curiosity, out of ignorance, or simply we just learn it, whatever the circumstance that brought us in to a road of pain, with the same attitude and decision we could break it, cold turkey, is just a decision to be free to a better you, they say a journey of a thousand miles starts with the first step and then another until we get there, is just like that with everything we do, is just a decision make up your mind and do it, pray and don't cease praying, exercise to keep your mind busy, read to get stronger, listen to audio books, if the friends we hang out with are part of the problem change your friends if you grow bigger your friends will stay behind, likeminded people attract the same kind of people, is a law, when we slowly start breaking from those chains we will know if we really got rid of them, and are no longer there, when in temptation of our weakness we are strong enough and succeed walking away, as for every weakness of the heart you would be tempt over and over until you no longer feel the weakness, it will disappear forever if we walk away constantly, it is an eternal fight for territory of good and evil and inside of us, when Jesus say "the ax is already at the root of the trees" he also meant to say his word is the ax that could help eliminate all of our problems away, at the very root but our commitment to change most come with a willing discipline to get in the habit and never surrender and feed our spiritual life with the scripture, even if we start with small baby steps, eventually we will become strong readers and our wisdom will come naturally, and best of all, a strong force will grow to help us abandon all our enemies inside, that have been keeping us slaves for so much time.

Every day when we wake up we get a new opportunity to change and become better or remain the same over and over for as long as we want, keep having the same attitude about life, about everything that surrounds our little own world, or expand and feel part of a bigger plan and work to accomplish better things inside and out, we all want to move on and move up, become better and get better, we all need the same spiritual strength to fight for territory inside our own amazing and complex body. One day we would run out of opportunities as we have to go and abandon this place forever when we die, we tend to think is far or never really expect it to come, but is inevitable one day we just won't have any more time to mature in our so immature soul, and death is the most accurate prove we have, we are not here just for the material things and possessions we own, or for the physical bodies we could have, we are here for the pure and unique experience of a spiritual learning, spiritual growth.

That which is attractive to our heart is what the enemy utilize to attract us and temp us, for as long as we are alive we will be able to get free if we really wish so, nothing is more powerful than the power of our own will when we have the determination to do something, when we give everything we got, and this enemy inside that is preventing us from living a plentiful life, full of all those blessings we cannot buy and are only acquired when you are at peace within and others, when we live according to the rules of the eternal, things just seem to be easy we get to sleep and walk with a clean conscious, we become like a white piece of paper where our life can be rewritten and start from scratch, and on this second part of our life we will entirely do what we really want and not what the enemy is forcing us to do, and that is, to see the darkest part of all of us get darker, where we constantly get depress, sad or angry and bitter, where we make enemies everywhere we go, and where we are judging or utilizing our tongue to destroy, to criticize, to show who we really are inside, as from the abundance of the heart speaks our mouth, this mouth that many times does not stop once it gets rolling, has cause many times our own destruction if we could just silence it as much as we possibly can, we want attention we speak, we want to give our opinion even when not one is asking, we lie, we talk just because is like a lose snake ready to bite, how difficult is to keep it shut, but as we learn and grow we will, if we can keep silence more and more, it's a sign we are growing.

To know and to comprehend internally who we are, requires to be, very alert mentally and in constant observation, how can I expect to know others when I don't know myself? If there is a confusion internally we could never have peace, we may think we are normal, but if we inflict pain to others and ourselves we are inconsistent, it shows our weakness, we need to know what they are, and set a target to find ways to fight it, to overcome this serious chain that holds our entire life to the same thing over and over we have to look at it straight and fight to get our freedom and break from it, as our destiny would depend on it, we have the obligation, we owed to ourselves, we owed to our love ones, but more importantly we owed to the eternal creator as our entire life we had turn our back in shame and pain away from him, we made the wrong turn at some point in our life, there is according to scripture only one who never made any wrong Jesus, as for the rest of us, we had, we are, or we will, this is why his message is so powerful to help us break with the impossible, if you could believe this with all your heart there is no doubt you will succeed, our words are powerful but the power of Jesus words are life and give life; it is not just possible but is a fact we could become a much better person one day at time, and after we find who or what the enemy is, the best way to start fighting is with a prayer from the very bottom of our heart, as this kind of prayer goes directly to our creator, he is been waiting patiently for this prayer since we abandon the correct path, and once we pray, we can be certain that we would have the strength to fight and be victorious in this fight as we will not be fighting alone, our Lord who wishes for each and every one to join in, the big family is waiting for us with a big smile and his arms wide open calling our names, as we surrender to him totally, in complete submission one can be certain you won't absolutely be alone anymore, we probably hear this many times but is true there are countless amount of people whose lives and transformation has been shocking after they submitted their entire existence to God their results are according to the faith and trust they use, and if this results are always positive why not trying, to follow Jesus is hard but if you don't is even more difficult, just start reading the gospels nothing else.

I personally fought many enemies, they were permanent tenants, living very comfortable inside my body, this temple of the Lord has been profaned but each and every one of those enemies was slowly been evicted a better person shortly was taking shape, they were some tenants perhaps since very early in my life, a mansion was built for the oldest tenants, and there were many times I thought I would die with all my bad enemies inside, as I saw them so much bigger and stronger than me, they did not leave without a fierce fight but I know for certain, the eternal was calling me to a transformation and this fight was also his, and I'm so grateful for his intervention as of today he keeps guard on my door and I have to make sure the footings of his building are getting more strength and the doors are constantly been renew and closed with the power and labor from his scripture and prayer, the way you open a door is committing sin with plain knowledge of what we doing, in reality I wish I could say it is an easy journey but is not, is full of pain and tears where we must relay completely in hope and faith, sometimes just waiting for the sun of the next day to bring light and hope to win our eternal fight for territory inside our temple.

I would not be able to write of something I have not experienced if it wasn't for his calling, there is a time in each one of us when our name is been called from above to come back in our senses and if we don't, his back might turn on us, his calling is forever until we decide to come, and if we reject the call, walking alone in life may be a very frightening time as we would completely be at the hands of the enemy of all creation, guiding us, and from that moment due to our bad actions eternal consequences. Forces are fighting for territory but the easy choice is likely wrongdoing, as the path of good comes with a feeling of loneliness and out of place, this path is uphill and full of obstacles and suffering, but most things good in life are worth every pain, every time we suffer, every tear, we grow a little more if you ask someone who has run a successful business or a success history often came with a lot of pain and obstacles but a determination and a strong will to always stay put, our success inside depends on a determined mind and a strong heart, but if we are lazy and comfortable we will never know the joy of beating those enemies whose tentacles obstruct our vision and darken our heart, to keep us blind and live in total darkness, this is true as the kingdom of the light does not belong here on earth.

PERSEVERENCE

Blessed is the one who perseveres under trial because,
having stood the test, that person will receive the crown
of life that the Lord has promised to those who love him.
James 1:12

As the flowers bloom in spring over and over, year after year for thousands
of years, the wildflowers on the empty fields, the mountains, the plants,
the trees, the rivers, the lakes, the oceans, the rain its nature at work to
keep the world in balance, and how the architect of the Universe idea of
continuous life and the renewal of hope to make everything new including
our spirit. As strong as we think we may be, we can never be prepared for
defeat, for tragedy, for the adversity that could knock on our door, is in
those times, we realize how vulnerable is our condition, we may look for
peace but it would run away from us like a butterfly, we can quite catch it,
we may look for a little joy but nothing is fun anymore, we may hunt for
light but everything might be dark, and if we see the rainbow

From our perspective it will look gray, our sadness and sorrow could
blind us and make it look darker than the vast ocean, We question our life
and existence; did we have a reason to exist? Why are we here? We may
have a lot more questions than we ever have in our entire life, and not an
answer for any of them, we may scream and the echo of our voice is the
only answer we get, our eyes may be dry of so much crying, our body is
weak, and our mind is like a blank piece of paper, just empty...

This is the moment you have been preparing all your life for, all of the small and big circumstances that happen in our life up until that moment, we're setting the stage for our "moment of true reflection and trial" we may never understand why? Perhaps is not for us to understand. Laying there on the floor at the lowest point in our existence, we should release this heavy load to the one who knows all the answers, the one who knows how? and why? He has been there our entire life, right in the very same place our pitiful body is breaking down.

Our creator is inside, he can hear every whisper, every heartbeat, and every thought in our head, and in fact, he feels our pain too, when his most precious son was suffering at the moment of trial, in his last moments of prayer before his crucifixion, Jesus prays several times and the Father heard every prayer but in his wisdom, he knew this was the best way to send a message to the world, although the Father was in terrible pain, even with the mighty power he didn't want to interfere with his big plan of love even after all possible hostility to his beloved son, one of the biggest lessons to humanity, "obedience" and "trust" in his wisdom as the suffering in the flesh is only temporary. When our forefathers sin by disobeying God's law "no to eat from the forbidden fruit" they transgress the law and someone have to pay the price of such disobedience or we would never be able to be at peace with GOD. For all of us is very difficult to understand love as the invisible bond of the Universe that God created, we love those close to us, the ones we share our life with, the ones who touch our spirit, and even with all the intensity we can love others, is nothing compare to the love our Father has for all His creation and in a very special way for humanity even with all our faults, under any circumstances the architect, the engineer, the designer, and the laborer of the Universe know and dwells inside every human on this planet, he feels a deep love for all of us, we could just never understand how much, is beyond imagination. Why we suffer, perhaps we never understand the biggest plan behind our suffering, but if we want to live with him we must trust, when we are weak, as his wisdom is perfect, we have to learn obedience, trust, and develop our faith, behind every night there is always a new day for thousands of years is been this way, and just when the night gets darker is when the sunlight is about to come, it never fails, it is another sign of hope as just when our problems are at worst the sun of new opportunities, a new life a new person would come out all our bad circumstances and troubles, it never fails. Adversity has a way to touch every soul at some point in our lifetime but behind hidden is always a big lesson, we otherwise could never learn any other way, before we get to this point in our life we must start preparing our inner spiritual life to be able to handle any situation or circumstance better, otherwise, if we don't, we may fall in deep depression and obscure thoughts, there is no magic recipe to handle adversity but there is a cushion we can build for when we fall and it won't be as hurtful, and this cushion is our spiritual life.

We are obligated to unload this heavy load from our shoulders, if a heavy burden rest inside, we could cry to empty our pain and get to rest, get up and admire the small detail in nature a sunrise, the wind whispering on the treetops, the hard-working come and go of the small working ants, the falling of the rain or the snow, the flowers, the sand, the water, the ocean, the flying of the birds, the clouds, the starts, or the leaves falling as the wind take them on a free ride, or a simple spider web, enjoy this moment for as long as you need, and realize how God plan was always perfect we were meant to be as harmonious as everything else in nature but when the first human on earth disobey, we mark our destiny and it was our choice to engage against nature and the harmony of life following the very principles and rules that surround and govern every creature in the Universe.

Don't be ungrateful just look at your surroundings it took thousands of years to build all those amazing places on earth your eyes can admire, it took hundreds of years for you to have all the comfort and luxury around you, the ready available water, the condiments for our meals, a toilet with water, airplanes, electricity, TV, radio, internet, cellphones, transportation and very comfortable shoes, ready and available meals, hearing and vision devices for us to see and hear better, the ability to take care of our teeth, and much, much, much more we could fill many books describing, all those amazing things we take for granted is very natural to get used to and forget our comfortable surroundings, that alone is a reason to be full of gratitude and if we are humble enough to understand the many miracles we have, the ones we get for free but could not buy even if we are rich, each one have a different share of this miracles but since they were free we just simply take them for granted and never appreciate, imagine if for any weird circumstance you end up in jail tomorrow, after some time been deprived of your freedom you will treasure how incredible is, just been free even if you don't have anything else, all of a sudden freedom becomes priceless.

If we have a roof every night and at least a meal every day, we could fill our hearts with gratitude, just as thousands of people lived their entire lives without all of these luxuries and more for centuries.

Since the creation of men, hardship is part of our never-ending learning experiences, on one hand, we would have many blessings every day in our life, on the other hand, the struggle, the problems, and sufferings, we must bury them but not in the heart, we should dig a hole and plant them outside and never water them, we don't have to let those struggles sufferings and problems grow, we can't water them every time because they will grow to the point where our existence orbits around them, they create a burden and a hole inside, a deep sadness, we could live a life with all the adversity around us, without getting into us if only we learn to put them in a different perspective as we tend to give problems more power than they deserve if something or someone controls you is only because you give them power.

If our last day is tomorrow and we assume is true, would all the adversity have the same meaning? Does it have the same weight? What would hurt more? the problems we leave behind or the fact that everything would end tomorrow, all our dreams, our hopes, our loved ones, how much would they miss you, the struggle, perhaps all those things we dream about once, perhaps all those things we accomplish and fight so hard to get, all our life will now become dust, because our departure from this planet is imminent, this somber thought is a true statement, "one day tomorrow is your last day" I can assure this is true as the fact we all have the power to make everyday a much better day if we accept the message of Jesus in our everyday life, a hopeful and peaceful day could be today and if we push it, could become very good day; why? Because this message has the promises if we believe with faith a peaceful, joyful, and eternal life awaits.

Every single worry would be no more heavyweight on your last day, every concern would stay here with the shadow of your existence, are we ready to go today?. It's not worth it, to live with all the pain and suffering, as we are just a moment, realize that all of it was just to learn, to grow, to move on, to mature, to change, to be better, in the future it will all work out for the best, as everything in this planet does, everything pass and gives way to something new, our Father knows what is best all the time, every time, it is a law of nature everything changes giving birth to something new or something better, persons, opportunities, and circumstances would slowly appear that otherwise never would.

And as we all have a date with death, we must take seriously every single day and value the priceless commodity "time", like a precious glass of water when we are thirsty, or like a good meal when we are hungry. Yesterday as I was driving on the way to work, I saw an accident that shock me, as the SUV was upside down and the passenger door on the ground, by the median of the highway, I remember, what hit me hard was to see the whole top of the car was pushed down flat against the truck seats, I wonder if those persons involved in the accident where ready to go, nobody is, we are never really ready, like you and me, we wake up every morning thinking about everything we have to do, our worries, concerns never even thinking for one second this is my last day, I'm not coming back, we never do that, we shouldn't, but it is important every night before we rest, to reconcile with our creator and to deposit our fights and struggles on his hands.

This small gesture of humility increases our spiritual strength as we deposit what we can't do or fix on to the one who can, we deposit what we fear on the invincible almighty all-powerful, we deposit our offenses on the merciful, we deposit our problems on the wise, we deposit our pain on the healer, we can only walk a step a at time, we can only live one day at a time, deposit and feed your spirit to prepare for the last trip. Is not hard to do it, just takes some will and a few minutes even when we are exhausted it is perhaps a small good investment as we deposit all we have and all we are, trust we are in good hands. prayer is not only to heal but protection and if we bless our kids and pray for them we are doing more for them than we can imagine, we have to trust and have faith this small token of love recognizing our limits and fragility is the key to the kingdom of heaven Jesus always talked about, faith is, believing with hope, what we can't see.

But as it is written, What no eye has seen, no ear has heard, and no human heart has conceived— God has prepared these things for those who love him. 1 Corinthians 2:9.

This brings me up to another important point, always live the present moment, many people if not all of us are always rushing to the next thing we have to do and forget the small moment, every single clip of life we live will never come back again; if we are seating to have dinner and have our family together, we chat for some time, but never the same moment of life would repeat, once finish is gone forever, every moment of the present time is precious and we have to treasure it, take mental pictures and real pictures, have your full attention to the moment is important! Don't rush your life and especially if you are just running to do the never-ending chores, family is more important. What I want to express is the fact that we cannot go on like if we are to be eternal, living in this planet like if tomorrow is guaranteed and this a tendency the majority of people has and we avoid thinking about our departure but is not helping, it gives you a sense of security and we think, I'll do it tomorrow, I'll do it next year, I won't forget, I won't forgive, I don't have to apologize, but if we realize the present is today and tomorrow might never come, would you apologize? Would you go out and enjoy, and do many, many different things that otherwise we would just keep postponing, thinking we have many years to live yet, we have time, people who have been in prison for a long time learn to appreciate freedom, people who are terminally ill learn to appreciate health and love every day with joy, why wait? Why not today? Why postpone our dreams, is true we cannot think about death all the time but we have to go on, every day as if today was the last one, just to be healthy conscious, there has been people I lost along the way and I wish they were here just one more day, many times I had the opportunity to call, to write a letter and then one day you realize they are gone forever, many times I wish I had travel more instead of working so much, we have become the new age slaves we just work and work and work so much to keep up with our life style and to pay bills and we forget to work to live and not live to work, finding a balance is difficult specially when we have so much responsibility, but starting up with small things to break the routine and make life more interesting, rather than just giving one hundred percent to our jobs and fifteen percent to our families, our jobs one day will replace us, but our family is always there even after many jobs, we need to get our priorities straight and keep a good balance we will not remember our memories at work as much as the ones at home.

The Rich Man and Lazarus

"There was a rich man who was dressed in purple and fine linen and lived in luxury every day. 20 At his gate was laid a beggar named Lazarus, covered with sores 21 and longing to eat what fell from the rich man's table. Even the dogs came and licked his sores.

"The time came when the beggar died and the angels carried him to Abraham's side. The rich man also died and was buried. 23 In Hades, where he was in torment, he looked up and saw Abraham far away, with Lazarus by his side. 24 So he called to him, 'Father Abraham, have pity on me and send Lazarus to dip the tip of his finger in water and cool my tongue, because I am in agony in this fire.'

"But Abraham replied, 'Son, remember that in your lifetime you received your good things, while Lazarus received bad things, but now he is comforted here and you are in agony. 26 And besides all this, between us and you a great chasm has been set in place, so that those who want to go from here to you cannot, nor can anyone cross over from there to us.'

"He answered, 'Then I beg you, father, send Lazarus to my family, 28 for I have five brothers. Let him warn them, so that they will not also come to this place of torment.'

"Abraham replied, 'They have Moses and the Prophets; let them listen to them.'

"'No, father Abraham,' he said, 'but if someone from the dead goes to them, they will repent.'

"He said to him, 'If they do not listen to Moses and the Prophets, they will not be convinced even if someone rises from the dead.'"

Luke 16:19-31

We have the ability to make our life a better place for us and others, we just have to trust and have faith, if we get better and try to live a life full of hope, all those around us would feel touch, this is a good way to spread the life of a true Christian. In this life we go through many ordeals and challenges and get many opportunities to grow and help others, and if we grow something good inside, out of some adversity, just like a seed we put on the ground, it has to die to become something better and multiply, it will transform to a plant, a flower or a tree, a tragedy is not meant to destroy us, is a new beginning if only time could show us what good would come out of this despair if only we could see, it was for the best and the better, we don't have the wisdom to understand, we don't have the whole picture in our very limited vision, we can't see past our present time and we will not grow if we knew. Many times the things we do or say affect someone for the rest of their lives just like that, our deeds are the little creations we go on spreading around, this is why is so important to grow spiritually to change for the better and build a better world, to touch others and lead them the right way, help them when everyone else is pointing fingers, help them when everyone else turns their backs when something bad happens to us and instead of channeling this trough the filters of faith and hope we grow bitter and then we go on spreading our bitterness and anger around, our little world is going to feel like a battleground where we have to have a weapon ready and live hidden in a trench and if someone approaches we are on the defensive ready to shoot and kill, how many victims of this behavior are killed like this in this world? We kill them with our bitterness and many times we create monsters because those around us too often are many times our reflection especially if we are leaders in our homes, our surroundings began to reflect sooner than later what we are and that is exactly what we attract if you want to know who you are, take a look at the ones that surround you all the time, the ones who you spend a lot of time with if you are an intellectual probably your friends are similar to you if you are a mobster more likely your friends are just like you, if you hear a lot of gossip from others, you get my point, you cannot attract what is not similar to you because you would not feel comfortable, this is an eye-opener to see a little into who we are, we have to ask the question, are we building this world by helping others with our words? Or are we destroying them? Your words are powerful, use them wisely, words either build or destroy and if what we talk is poison is best to keep our mouth closed.

There is a story of an old man, his son, and two mares, they lived in a small town and used the animals to carry wood and to work the land, to survive they sold the wood and used the mares to plow the fields they planted, one day the two mares scape and the town was a small place and everybody knew each other, they heard the news about the scape and came to tell the men how sorry they were and how big was their disgrace, the old man would just nod and said perhaps.

A month went by and the two mares came back pregnant and they brought two wild horses with them, the whole town was so happy and came to tell him he was very blessed because now he had four horses and two more were coming since they were pregnant.

One day while his son was domesticating the wild horses, he fell from one of them and broke his arm and a leg, the whole town came quickly to tell the old men they were sorry for him and how big was his disgrace, the old men would just nod and said perhaps.

Two weeks later, a civil war broke in and the army came in to recruit every man in town who was able to bear arms, they took all of the young men of the town, and the whole town, later on, came to tell the men how fortunate he was, his son was not able to go to war, the old men just nod and said perhaps.

Sometime after that, the son heal and he fell in love and marry the most beautiful woman in town, as usual, the whole town came to tell the old men how fortunate his son was, the old men just nod and said perhaps, a year went by and the beautiful woman became very sick, she lost weight and was almost dying, everyone knew she might die and the whole town came to tell the old men they were sorry and how great was his disgrace, the old men just nod and said perhaps, sometime after that rebels were running and came to town at night and rape a lot of women in town when they knock down his door, they saw the ill woman and they left.

Sometime after that, the old man was dying and before he pass, he told his son "do never get too happy when you receive a blessing and when everything is going well" and also "do never get too sad and worry when tragedy and pain come in" for as long as you always do the right thing,

God the highest of the Universe would always be looking out for you, "be at peace in the joy," "be at peace in the pain," enjoy just one day at a time.

We did not come to this world to rest and drink on the beach, to party and play, for as much as we wish, it's not the purpose, probably that part of the big plan, is reserved for another place in the unlimited universe of the creator but definitely not here, if we party and enjoy for a long time, life will push you, and toss you around and upside down, for it is in adversity, pain, and trouble we grow.

Circumstances happen to make a better you after pain we need to be resilient, we would be knocked down but we should never stay down, we could get beat but we shall never give in, our body is just like everything else in nature it is self-reconstructed, after destruction, after a wildfire, everything is born again after a volcano erupts everything becomes more fertile, after a storm comes the most beautiful day ever, and spiritually and physically is not different from everything else in nature is just time, time is the key. We are definitely explorers, we are not on a vacation in this journey we call life, if you are a tourist everything is planned and everything is fun, we eat, we drink, we have fun, and never worry about tomorrow, we just enjoy the moment, but if we are explorers then we enter on a wild territory where we don't know what or where we going and how is going to end, how we are going to eat, and what, the danger of tomorrow would be, therefore we become more prepared more aware of the wild animals, the dangers of the jungle and the desert, we learn to create fire as we know fire is a key component to survive in the wild, we sleep, aware of the dangers that are lurking all the time, and we learn to survive with pain and struggle and if we are able to survive until we age we would then be consider blessed; we come to be explorers our faith is the fire and the same way we struggle to learn how to make a fire for a long time in the beginning the same way is the spark of faith, and the wild is the world with all the danger, but if we live our life as tourists on a vacation trip, what would we learn? We would not be prepared when the unexpected comes, how would we survive without fire for the darkness.

THE RUDDER

Our body is the slave of our mind, if we believe we are weak, we are, if we believe we are strong it helps us get stronger, there are remarkable stories of the infinite strength of our mind, it is what makes us different from the animal kingdom and is always growing until the day we die, who can deny we have a very powerful, complex and sophisticated mind, and we have the blessing out of all the creatures on earth to be able to expand it and use it; if we use it or not, the potential is there.

Here are some examples of true stories:

In one case in Colorado in 1995 a police officer arrived at a single-car accident where a Chevette ended up on top of a baby girl and sank in the mud, the officer lifted the car and the mother pull the little girl out.

In 2009 a man in Kansas lifted a Mercury sedan off a six-year-old girl who had been trapped underneath when it back out on top of her.

In 1960 a Florida mom lifted a Chevy impala so that a neighbor could pull out her son, who had become trapped when he was working on the car and his jack collapsed.

And the case where an MD500D helicopter crashed in 1998, pinning the pilot under shallow water; and his burly fiend (nickname tiny) ran over and lifted the one-ton helicopter enough for the pilot to be pulled out.

These are just a few, from countless examples of human strength under extraordinary circumstances. But there are more stories of resilience as every one of us has a story, we could write a book about every person trials and difficulties in life, but also when we are struck with adversity, tragedy, and pain, we could use this strength in reverse; the same kind of strength to help us survive could also submerge us in deep pain and hurt us badly, it happens very often when we fall on depression.

And the countless times our mind has been used for the wellbeing of humanity, to progress, the unlimited inventions that change our world forever. It's so powerful that if we only knew how much, our respect for this amazing creation we carry around in our head would be very profound.

We are so bless to have the freedom and ability to turn our mind into whatever creation we want, but this freedom can be misleading and very costly, as if we turn all of our attention and concentration to wrong doing consciously or unconsciously sooner or later we will pay the price with pain, with tears, with blood, or jail, for a short time or for a long time and all this pain can be avoided if we always walk the straight line of a good human behavior, following the example of all nature as everything in nature obeys God instructions, they are simple, but our judgment could be mistaken to discern, right from wrong as if someone hurt us, the natural response of the human judgment would be to retaliate, resentment and anger would surface, but our Lord ask us to forgive and don't keep any hard feelings about it; but how difficult is for us to understand the power and mercy of God, in our very thin understanding we only see the moment the instant and our ego push us to believe we can make justice and give everyone who mistreat us or hurt us a payback, one reason middle east is always at war is because they don't understand forgiveness, this was a big part of the good news Jesus promoted; God ask us to trust, to realize he has the power to give, to take away, to forgive, to do justice, to create, to destroy, to life and to death, with this almighty power everything is under his direct supervision and nothing would be forgotten if we don't repent while we are alive, but if I offended God hurting others and my arrogance blinds my eyes my pride hardens my heart, and continue walking this path until I die, our judgment could be very strict.

And how terrible must be, to be in front of the tribunal of God, knowing how much we offended him and turn our back to him, besides all the opportunities we had every day of our lives to walk his path and to repent, the path he traced for every one of us, but we complicate our existence by confusing freedom with internal anarchy, our mind is in total control of life or self-destruction is our rudder.

There is a consequence of everything we do, while we are alive there are laws we must obey according to where we live if we break the law we must pay, in the spiritual world there are laws our Lord commanded and if we break them there will be consequences the result no one knows only our creator.

> Jesus himself told us "he is not God of the dead, but the living" Mark 12:27

when Jesus refers to Abraham, Isaac, and Jacob been alive, he is making a statement of the existence of people already dead in an afterlife, a God of the living, as we with certainty will face the proper judgment of all our actions, and how scary is this thought, if you ever been in a courtroom the feeling inside is very intimidating and if we are on the accusation stand it must be terrifying, and that is, here on earth, now imagine in front of the one who has seen all of our thoughts and actions and has the total power of our eternity, it is incomprehensible for us to even understand what eternity is, and how small we are, my point is to use your rudder for good steering in all circumstances.

That's why our freedom has to be used to create, to help, to grow, to do better for ourselves and others, to serve, and many other useful things that we could honor our freedom and to glorify God who gave us the free will, and always be very conscious of the very thin line between good and bad. Our mind, our eternal director in the things we do, when we feed it with the wrong information can completely take us far from the truth, pride would blind us and arrogance would harden our heart, is the right formula to bring us to a life full of mistakes as we tend to move without direction or control, even when we think we have control, I can easily feel related to this description as I walked a good part of my life with the wrong information feeding my mind, therefore the wrong results all the time, there was a time when I felt invisible and would look for a fight for no reason, there was a time when I was promiscuous, there was a time when I thought I knew everything and in my mind, everything was so easy, there was a time when a stranger was a stranger his problems and his worries were his and not mine, there was a time when God was sometimes in my mind, but far away from my heart a cold selfish heart.

If we decide to start a change after we direct our mind to do it we have to ask for help first from God, second, if we have a good friend you trust and is even better if he had accepted God in his heart or perhaps someone you know who change drastically for the better It is very difficult or impossible to fight alone for the simple reason we are weak even when we have a desire to change we always need help.

"Watch and pray so that you will not enter into temptation. For the spirit is willing but the body is weak" Matthew 26:41

If there is one thing that I am certain, is my immense ability and creativity to sin, and all my brothers and sisters in this world share these skills with me, we must be humble enough to realize we can't get out of it alone, we need help, all the time, everywhere, praying should be our spiritual food to continue with all the challenges of everyday life, if we are constant and discipline in our prayers, the strength we earn to fight is powerful, and those battles are no longer ours.

The recipe to our only hope of true change is in these words of Jesus when he prayed at Gethsemane, watch and pray so that you will not enter into temptation, our weakness is only strong when we are alone when the fight is only our fight we would probably be defeated many times over and over, only when we look for help from above these fights are no longer ours and the probabilities of success are substantial, how do we find and direct our mind and soul to the help readily available to anyone? The word of God even if we feel we are in the worst of any human condition, the word has power and the message is an individual message to each and every one

"Wash and make yourselves clean. Take your evil deeds
out of my sight; stop doing wrong." Isaiah 1:16

The mercy of God is immense and if we look for him slowly like a baby learning to walk, slowly our change would follow.

"Learn to do right; seek justice. Defend the oppressed. Take up the cause of the fatherless; plead the case of the widow." Isaiah 1:17

The reward has not price, is many times greater than all the riches in the world: "Come now, let us settle the matter says the Lord "Though your sins are like scarlet, they shall be as white as snow; though they are red as crimson, they shall be like wool. Isaiah 1:18

We can direct our mind to the right information if we really look for it, if you are reading this and you have gotten this far, you might be seeking for some sense in to your life, or you are all looking for direction, I hope you find the little seed, that would soon grow into a three, the word of God in reality is a bath, a refreshing shower in our dirty and unstable condition, a life saver in a wild stormy sea when we are about to be drown, if our conscious is screaming for help, we can still be saved, but just like an arm with gangrene if our conscious is already too quiet, when or after we do wrong and we feel not more pain or remorse, the limb is dead it has to be cut off, just like that, we could be lost, there is nothing worse than a cold heart it has so much anesthesia due to our blindness and toxic mind, don't allow one more day with so much burden, liberate your mind and enrich your spirit, having a broken rudder would have you wandering in the ocean of life and possibly ending where you never meant to be or drowning in the middle of a storm, or simple lost. Is our responsibility to pray for those who are cold-hearted and non-believers, is a small act of mercy.

HIS STEPS

When we wake up in the morning at a nice sunny day and we go on with our everyday chores, we don't think about anything other than the things we have to do on that day, the things we did yesterday and the goals we have for tomorrow, we are concentrated in our own little world and everything else is secondary, is others who are in war, is others who are sick, is others who are suffering, is other people who are hungry, is other people who can't afford the basic things just to make ends meet, but when we suffer we demand sympathy, in our heart we wish others would understand and feel for us, and is precisely when we suffer that our sympathy for others who suffer grows and touch us deep to help us grow, we begin to be more sensible, that is one more reason suffering is a step to spiritual growth, even when none of us want to suffer is a necessity in this every day battle we call life, how many times you hear stories from someone who was born financially free and they never suffer, many are cold hearted and they don't care at all for others, not understanding pain is difficult until you are in it. Is very difficult to understand pain if we never felt what pain is like, if we were to live in a world full of abundance and happiness we would lose perception of reality as this world is not like that, there is always a road full of hurdles, there is pain and heartache as we already know and the more we get the more we grow spiritually, we realize how vulnerable we are, but is not the only way to grow, those who become friends with Jesus from early in life experience growth and pain, but with the pain comes a spiritual reward.

Many parents want to prevent pain and suffering on their kids is an instinct natural to do this and is completely normal but exaggerated and constant overprotection is doing more damage than good as this makes kids lose perception of what the world is, and they may become insensible too, to the pain and need of others. I wish my kids didn't have to suffer I know this is not the case they will suffer but even if they had experienced some pain too, the only thing we can do is feed their minds, enrich their spirit and their hearts to prepare for the best but expect problems all alone their path, when we interact with other errant humans we can always expect all kinds of problems and how difficult is to find a stable mind and a big heart, you see, this is why we are obligated to improve, for us, for them, for the world.

Since the day we were born our entire life is a challenge it is a constant and never-ending battle, the battle even Jesus himself had to endure as a man, as any other man been born on this planet, but unlike any other man before or after him, he came to this world full of wisdom, humility and truth, he endures all the pain and humiliation possible, he stayed humble and at peace, he knew the ordeal was just temporary, as painful and horrible his death was, he knew his death was going to make better humanity as it had never existed before him, he came to reveal the truth for all of us to know, to be saved, his words were not the only proof, it was his work his miracles, as no other man before or after him, gave us so many signs, he had the power to heal hundreds of people who came to him, but also have the power to resurrect from the dead to some people who died in his three years of preaching and teaching. And his resurrection, where hundreds witnessed his glory and they believed, how rich and beautiful experience of a life-changing; we could say if I could only see him the same way they did, if I lived during that time, I would be more faithful I would trust, I would know is true, as a matter of fact for Jesus and our Father it was very easy to convert the whole world in a second, to show them his glory, but our Father wants to be loved by free will, by pure love the same way we love our biological mother, father, sons, and daughters, and we are probably thinking, but I can't see God! Nobody loves what you don't know, and much less what we can see, but Jesus said:

"I am the way, and the truth, and the life. No one
comes to the Father except through me. *John 14:6*

Jesus told his disciples this true, for the future generations to understand
Jesus is like a compass, inviting us to know him, to get to the father, to
understand what is required from us we have to study his words, his
actions, and his work, if I want to go to a far city or any place in the world,
I need a road, a path, a direction, a map and to get there, I need to follow
the map to the tee or I would end up somewhere else, is a simple way to
understand a little about the meaning of this phrase, if he is the way the
truth and the life, why I am looking everywhere else for a direction but
not Jesus? Where is the common sense in my search? Is this why we don't
have a life? We follow every other way, any other truth, many theories,
and we end up confused, dead inside and we find consolation in drugs,
consolation in pleasure, and anything else, but always empty and lonely.

Today more than ever before in history we need a path, the roads to
perdition are way too many, how can you explain to a kid God is the same
yesterday today and tomorrow he is not old fashion, they love so much
video games and science fiction, if they could only see we have a God who
can divide the ocean in two parts, we have a God who can walk on water,
we have a God that commands all the starts of the Universe, a God who
has an army of powerful angels where one of them can kill thousands of
men in seconds, we have a God that could make a water fountain from
a rock in the middle of a desert, a God that would make a fire without
burning nothing, a God that could create food to fall from the clouds like
rain to eat, we have a God that commands insects to destroy all vegetation
if he wishes to, we have a God who owns chariots of fire, we have a God
who's angels are invisible and powerful they may, if commanded become
visible, we have a God who can make a rain of fire to destroy a city like
the ancient Sodom, we have a God who could feed thousands multiplying
a piece of bread, we have a God who can make a sterile woman fertile, we
have a God that can cure any illness physical, physiological, or spiritual,
we have an abundant God who can give riches to whomever, we have a
God who can create everything new including you if you let him, we
have a God that is immortal, is eternal and ever present, we have a God
who's love is bigger than anything created, we have a God more powerful

83

than all of your wildest dreams you can imagine. If you were to create a mini robot with an sophisticated programing, capable of multiplying and increase their intelligence, and then you go away for a very long time but you are able to access all of their information through the program from wherever you are, and realize your creation was dazzling but after a time those robots are so self-sufficient and they do all sorts of unimaginable, and despicable things to hurt themselves and others as well as forgot the fact they were created and their ego blinds their simple reasoning, and now you the creator is an illusion they don't even acknowledge, but as the time goes further they become worst and worst, you are the creator and you have try to reprogram them but this glitch just keeps altering a lot of your work if you make an appearance they would be amaze and believe they were created but you rather let them live with freedom because you understand individualism helps them grow, this for the guy who likes fiction is amazing imagination, well I got news for you this almighty and powerful God is real, as real as the air you breath and he can see inside your mind at all times.

All the ones who have started to follow the steps to encounter Jesus have the responsibility to introduce Jesus to other people's life and if they acknowledge him, our amazing Father will do the rest, we would feel a joy and peace as not one and nothing in the world could give you, his word is the truth and the truth opens our heart to a real purpose and the more we learn about Jesus the more we fall in love, just like when we fell in love for the first time and we couldn't do nothing without our love who always lived in our mind, just the same way, the more we know Jesus the more we fall in love and the more we talk about his love, his love is for real, as nobody could be capable of loving as much as the love of God, our love to others is convenient, opportunistic and many times false; when we fall in love we wouldn't dare to do anything that would hurt our love one to make them walk away from our life, we would behave accordingly to feel good and make our love proud, so they could love us more and trust us more, this is not different from the way we have to love Jesus, we would consciously walk without deviating to the left or to the right, we would try to walk a straight path knowing our love is aware of everything we do, everything we think, and everything we see, this is the kind of love that would make you beautiful and shine, it would make us radiant as the love of Jesus would be upon us. Others might notice and see right through your eyes a spark a shine, not different when people ask you, are you in love? If you want to shine, find Jesus love, many times is easy to find people in love; that glitter, that spark, the joy for living, the hopes and the dreams, and at the same time is fairly easy to find those who are fed up with life, those wrinkles in the face denote anger, those eyes deep with rage or in a derogative way, and here we get another another truth, everywhere we would find good people and not so good people, in every institution, in every group, is human nature and since the very beginning when one son of Eva kill the other, perhaps in the forbidden fruit the seed of evil runs inside and ever since some of us have more tendencies to evil than others, I wish I'm wrong but history don't lie, where there is two minds there is two wills this is why marriage is one of the most difficult partnerships it will take everything you have to make it work and in every group or association some more than others there is always selfishness, envy, gossip, back stabbing that tendency of talking about others when they are not around, even in places where you would think you'll never find this kind of behavior like a Church is always around, lurking in every corner to create frictions, problems, separations, hostility.

We all have the free will to love Jesus and we could choose not to, but if you don't who would you love then?, aside from your family there is always this void we need to fill, who would fill the place in your heart, that place in the heart has the shape of Jesus only he can fill that void, we were born full of emotions and we came to love, if the planet stop turning, the whole weather around the planet would collapse and if the sun flames would cease we would freeze to death, if the rain stops, we will have a drought we would perish, everything in this planet has a specific task to complete in order for life to be perpetual, but if any of the physical bodies small or big, falls short on those duties the consequences could be huge or small according to the task and the duration, when we fall short on loving, the planet suffers, evil in its many forms greed, pride, hate, revenge, lust etc. begin to grow, we inflate each day as toads with selfish love, we simply break the very first reason to exist therefor as with all other physical bodies when they stop doing their task death is the consequence, the same way when we don't love, death would be the result.

The same thing happened to Sonoma and Gomorrah their behavior and sins were so horrible to the eyes of our creator that he set an example destroying them, as the lack of love brings death, how much more can we expect when our behavior during this time is probably much worse by far than of those two ancient misfortune cities.

I often wonder why it was so hard for many people to believe in Jesus during his time when he lived among his people when they saw all of his works and signs when his personality was so radiant and his wisdom fathomless, Jesus himself told us one time, during one of his preaching's the answer to that question:

> And no one after drinking old wine wants new, for he
> says, "the old is better." Luke 5:39

Can we drink from the new wine? Are we ready to abandon our old ways, is never late for as long as we are alive we can, is a decision.

Any one used to the old ways and bad behavior could not accept his teachings even if they were eye witness to Jesus work, and this is true for anybody who at some point in their life come face to face with Jesus, we make a choice either we keep our old ways, bad habits and way of thinking the same attitude, or we change radically to the new teaching of the master and try to follow his path, his ways, not just by reading and attending church, but from the heart as talking about God and feeling and living God are two different things, as when we talk about God we could be brilliant, but our life could be far distance from God, and everything we do is far from good, or when we feel God presence and we behave as if we knew with certainty he is watching everything we do and listening to everything we say, and therefore we have a feeling of his presence, how much more difficult is for us in modern times to believe and accept his teachings as we lose perception of the truth and think we are self-made and self-sufficient, as all the glitter in the stage is set and ready since the day we are born, to recreate our eyes, to distract us, and to believe anything we want and everything anyone teaches, to deviate us from the truth; it is a job for all those who believe and have the certainty of God to help others find the path and the truth, there is an amazing promise in this regard:

"Remember this: Whoever turns a sinner from the error of their way will save them from death and cover over a multitude of sins" James 5:20.

This requires courage and a little tact to know when or where one can take the opportunity to bring the master teachings, what I found in my little experience is that my words are made of dust, they are easily taken by the wind but when I bring the scripture as is written, is like knives getting deep inside others and this is when the word of God starts working, nobody knows how but the word is a seed, even after we go this seed was planted and won't be easily removed from the heart sometimes after a long time we can find some change, much to our surprise, this duty was one of the first orders from Jesus when he appears to his apostles and during this times we feel inappropriate to talk about the scripture and many times we hold it inside because of fear, this is true but what I found many times is that we do a small silence prayer and much to our surprise once we start talking we realize everyone is hungry for this word of hope.

Jesus himself taught us in one of his preaching's this parable

The Parable of the Talents

"For it will be like a man going on a journey, who called his servants and entrusted to them his property. To one he gave five talents, to another two, to another one, to each according to his ability. Then he went away. 16He who had received the five talents went at once and traded with them, and he made five talents more. So also he who had the two talents made two talents more. But he who had received the one talent went and dug in the ground and hid his master's money. Now after a long time the master of those servants came and settled accounts with them. And he who had received the five talents came forward, bringing five talents more, saying, 'Master, you delivered to me five talents; here, I have made five talents more.' His master said to him, 'Well done, good and faithful servant. You have been faithful over a little; I will set you over much. Enter into the joy of your master.' And he also who had the two talents came forward, saying,

'Master, you delivered to me two talents; here, I have made two talents more.' His master said to him, 'Well done, good and faithful servant. You have been faithful over a little; I will set you over much. Enter into the joy of your master.' He also who had received the one talent came forward, saying, 'Master, I knew you to be a hard man, reaping where you did not sow, and gathering where you scattered no seed, so I was afraid, and I went and hid your talent in the ground. Here, you have what is yours.' But his master answered him, 'You wicked and slothful servant! You knew that I reap where I have not sown and gather where I scattered no seed? Then you ought to have invested my money with the bankers, and at my coming I should have received what was my own with interest. So take the talent from him and give it to him who has the ten talents. For to everyone who has will more be given, and he will have an abundance. But from the one who has not, even what he has will be taken away. And cast the worthless servant into the outer darkness. In that place there will be weeping and gnashing of teeth.' Matthew 25:14

Jesus was not talking about money or richest, as he doesn't care about that, even when he is an abundant God and plentiful, but a way to interpret this message is this, he might be talking about the people who are under your responsibility and trust, how many of those entrusted to you are you bringing back to God? None like the last servant, or we are returning all the ones he entrusted to us and more, back to God like the good servant, and that is exactly who we are, just servants either we serve God or we serve the enemy, there is no middle as if we think we are neutral we are just rejecting God, therefore, we are serving the enemy as well directly or indirectly, no one has any excuse after Jesus teachings because even when we can't visually see his works directly he left his message for everyone who wants a better life, for anyone tired, afflicted and exhausted from anyone who wants be saved from the enemy, he left his word and if this word comes to you, directly or indirectly and you turn around and head your old ways, you have no excuse anymore, we become like those who shout out load "crucify him" as those didn't believe either.

And to me it is countless times when I shout out loud "crucify him" but I'm so glad when he spoke to me one last time I listen because my life has been nothing but a new learning experience I had to let my old ways behind, my old way of talking, my old habits, my old thinking, and let the master fill my head with his teaching and my heart with his love, I was miserable who rejected Jesus for so long, and not because I didn't believe in him but because I lived like those Pharisees during Jesus time who sometimes would talk about God but whose hearts were far from the creator a hypocrite, and I don't have any doubt he gives us many opportunities to come back to him, I'm just so blessed to have accepted his truth before I depart from this world, it hasn't been easy, I wish from my heart all those who come across the word of Jesus one way or the other accept him and take the journey of fighting against the current, with pain but with a light spirit, and no matter what, as we go through all vicissitudes, Jesus would mold us into his disciples if we are open to listening, if our heart is open to true love, and if our eyes learn to see just good in everyone, like a little kid.

THE DARKNESS

As beautiful bright and glowing this world is; darkness is all around covering and taking over everything inside and out, this perpetual fight of light and darkness is truth, we are meant to be light, not shadows.

"The people living in darkness have seen a great light;
on those living in the land of the shadow of death a light
has dawned." Matthew 4:16

This prophesy as you know was Jesus birth, when Jesus was born he became the light this world saw for thirty-three years after he departed from this world, darkness came back but before he departed he left a small flame for all those who want to see in the darkness can find their way up to the celestial heaven and light their candles during their lifetime with his flame.

This invisible light that shines on those who follow, glorify God, and help us do the good deeds, this invisible light covers some of the deep darkness in this world, is the real light, faith, the word of God, the peace, the love, the hope, is everything that makes this life worth living, and of true value to a beautiful life, in the middle of this darkness.

God gave us his Son to show us the way back to him Jesus taught his wisdom to his disciples, to show the world what is waiting for them if they believe if we brighten our life with his teachings, how amazing it is to realize and to find out of the fathomless mercy of our creator to all of us, especially if we have been terrible sinners:

"I have not come to call the righteous, but sinners, to
repentance."
Luke 5:32

If we could only realize how fast life goes away, it seems like yesterday
when I was twenty, or twenty-five years old, it seems like time just has
flown and everything happen a couple of days ago and I know, one day if I
get to live my life to be seventy or eighty years old, all of a sudden is going
to feel like everything in life just happen the same way it has, we might
feel young but our body and face in the mirror would be a reality, time
just slipped by and we don't even notice, how short is our time, reconcile
with your creator, it's worth it, when we take a trip somewhere we follow
a road and we follow a direction you may get lost for a moment, but you
have a destiny, for certain any time you will get there, how difficult it is
to understand the spiritual and invisible world, how difficult is to firmly
believe, and even more difficult is to travel this road without direction or
path.

The invisible is just as real as the things we feel and the things we
touch if we could find our way back into the road we lost and the flame
we once killed.

When this little light of faith sparks inside, is our job to feed this fire
until it burns all of our bodies, on the other hand, when we let this light
disappear, we will be back to the world of darkness where death destroy
us, those men who wrote the scripture with the direction of the holy
spirit, confirm that life after we physically die is a fact, when we die in sin,
without repenting and without accepting Jesus, God may turn his back
forever and then this physical death is the beginning of our true death:

> "Yet you say, 'The way of the Lord is not just.' Hear,
> you Israelites: Is my way unjust? Is it not your ways that
> are unjust? 26 If a righteous person turns from their
> righteousness and commits sin, they will die for it; because
> of the sin they have committed they will die. *Ezekiel 18*

This death means before God you don't exist anymore, for an eternity
the lack of God, is true death, a full emptiness and in the spiritual would

be an eternal torment, and the word eternal does not have a complete understanding in our human mind, our brain can't grasp the truth meaning of eternal. "They will throw them into the blazing furnace, where there will be weeping and gnashing of teeth". (*Matthew 13:42*)

This world is in so much darkness and is because our own heart, our lack of love, empathy, and pain for others, is in darkness because we are feeding empty thoughts, personal and individual satisfaction, we dream to be on the spot light one way or the other, hearts get colder and more sinister than ever, we have abandon prayer and is in there the small act of prayer where we can make a big difference if we want to end wars pray, we want less violence pray, we want climate change pray, we want the perfect family pray, we want protection pray, where is your prayer? if you believe in Jesus why don't we pray, prayer is powerful even if you lack faith in your prayers, don't give up on them especially during the times where things go wrong because if you pray when you don't want you are doing a profound act of faith, in my personal experience when I started praying consistently every day and night and in between things started to go from bad to sometimes terrible, why? You may ask, because the enemy all good feels threatened and declares war on you, why because he is losing his grip on you and he wants you to desist and stop your prayers, and you are thinking but how come? Where is God? I can tell you, is right next to you because your fight is his fight and things would slowly get better for a much better life and your inner peace, pray because is your more fierce weapon; imagine a world where many people pray, imagine a city where everyone pray, imagine a house where everyone pray, we remember everything in our everyday life but prayer many times may not have any room during our days, the most essential thing is neglected, where are we going if we don't pray as a country, as a city, as a town, as a family as an individual, we are at the place where we are right now! a world full of darkness, perversion is everywhere at all levels, all kinds of spiritual cancers destroying all good, we read news and despicable acts that have not reason or meaning are happening, the darkness is really taking over the mind of too many people but we neglect to pray every year I can guarantee you less and less people pray, is not enough to be just a good person take action real action get on your knees and pray, insist on your prayers even when nothing is right and nothing seems to make sense, I hope we can turn this darkness with the light of prayer and good deeds, I wish this light grows and join many others who's together in this immense darkness would become a beacon of light for others to follow.

We should not go on, living afraid in the middle of these dark times but is the other way around we have to be aware of all the protection of our prayer and for the same reason live this life to the fullest, do what we have to, do what you must to improve, to get better inside and out, improve our attitude just this small gesture would improve our relationships, this is a beginning, small changes every week, every day, if you start praying and giving thanks is a small gesture of humility knowing your life is in best hands is a small change and change is what we need we all can improve a little all the time.

Is very important to teach our kids the importance of prayer and make them understand how important this is, it would be like giving them medicine but also preventive help, during this times we domesticate our kids but we don't educate them, now we feed them, we teach them manners, and is done, but sadly others are filling all the gaps and empty voids, we see kids coming from good families doing terrible things because they are learning from the dark places on the internet, we think oh well we are a good family, they have a roof and we feed them and take them to school we certainly expect good kids, maybe a hundred years ago, but not anymore, nowadays they have the whole world in their hands one wrong click and out of curiosity something evil gets in their fertile minds to be poisoned slowly, where are you? Minding your little world problems, then you are playing Russian roulette with your kids' minds, because if you don't feed their mind and spirit constantly there is a big chance something else could potentially feed their mind and spirit, they might come out as good kids and you will reduce the chances of been spirit poisoned if you get involved, we can't forget families are the main cell in our society, the more families destroyed the more problems as cities as a country, we are all in this and need to take action so good can overcome evil.

> "Which of you, if your son asks for bread, will give him a stone? Or if he asks for a fish, will give him a snake? If you, then, though you are evil, know how to give good gifts to your children, how much more will your Father

in heaven give good gifts to those who ask him! So in everything, do to others what you would have them do to you, for this sum up the Law and the Prophets". Matthew 7, 9-12

Just look around everywhere and realize how dark this world has become only if you are blind you won't see, nowadays kids can't walk alone on any street of the world without running into real danger from perverts who are lurking everywhere this exact thing happened during Sodom and Gomorra when on the day they were destroyed God sent two angels and they were disguise as foreigners and as soon as they walk in the city they were received by Lot at his home a big gang of men came to abduct this two foreigners to gang rape them, this is how sick their mind was already, and if you sum up the fact that all around the world kids alone are in danger think about how sick this world has become, nowadays adultery in all shape and forms is everywhere is like cancer or better yet like a covid-19 contagious is everywhere without even mentioning the liberty of sex and promiscuity without any conscious. Wake up and realize we are on the same day when these two ancient cities were destroyed we are just running out of time, do you think everything that has been happening around the world, the weather, the pandemic, volcanos, tsunamis, earthquakes, hunger, is all randomly? No, my brother no my sister we are past those ancient random times now is the tears of so much injustice that is claiming for justice, wake up get on your knees and pray while we still have time, maybe we might delay justice just one more day, but please don't be a fool justice is coming wake up! We have given satan more power than he never had before.

"Therefore keep watch, because you do not know on what day your Lord will come. But understand this: If the owner of the house had known at what time of night the thief was coming, he would have kept watch and would not have let his house be broken into. So you also must be ready, because the Son of Man will come at an hour when you do not expect him. Matthew 24, 42-44

BECOMING A CHILD

Why are children so beautiful and fun, why are children so capable of believing so easily? Smiling and laughing so easy, why are children so friendly? Why watch children play is a joy? Why do children love so easily? Why do children so easily forget the offense? Why they are so willing to learn? Why do their heartaches when they see the pain in others? Why they can make a good day out of any day? Why they don't worry about tomorrow? Why they are willing to help if we encourage them? Why do children hug so easily and love so easily? Why they are always willing to say the truth? Why do children see no evil? Because they lack evil, their heart is like a white sheet of paper, is light just like a feather, and empty to love and love some more. They only learn what we teach either good or bad. Yes, many children today know too much because they learn it, from their environment quickly but in general, this is the very nature of a child. When do we stop loving others, when did we stop being friendly, when did we stop believing, trusting, smiling, forgetting easy, and when did we stop making a good day with any circumstance, and then learn to lie so easy, to me it was the day I started to rationalize my thoughts and thinking, believing too easy on others was naive, smiling a lot was foolish, and been too friendly was daring, the way to survive and move around is to be an average adult, smile little, believe nothing, trust not one, judge others easy, over think everything and worry too much, losing faith easy because I didn't see a solution, giving up easy, and start having indecent thoughts, and thoughts are the babies of our actions, we simply part away slowly and without noticing away from our innocence, faith, from believing, from our ability to joy without reason at all, our ability to smile a lot and very easy, our ability to forget the offense as we recreate the offense over and over, as we torture ourselves to print this images until we live in a perpetual pain, and then an angry and bitter personality emerge, our own personal creation as victims of our own, over thinking and over reaction and recreation of things that hurt us and cut wounds in our hearts, as if we enjoy to feel like victims of every single thing that left a scar, we reason too much and our mind builds walls to restrict our emotions so people don't think we are too foolish, too silly and to fragile.

And later blame this pain on our present circumstances and our failures; we excuse our inability to forgive, reasoning on the seriousness of the matter, we blame the pain others inflicted, just because remembering is a way to excuse our present reality, to forget and to move on, just because we insist on holding up to a pain like our little doll, at night or when we remember we cry over it, and feel secure living with it, and the worst part of it, if we part from this world, with this negative and toxic feelings in our heart, the scripture says, "if we forgive others our Father in heaven would forgive us too"; Instead of taking the best and trashing the negative, the same way we do when we eat something we like, and has in it something we don't, we just don't eat what we don't like, why is so easy to forget the GOOD and so easy to remember the bad?, we can always say is not the same, is not easy, is a permanent scar, it might probably be and it will, but keeping it open and bleeding is just going to be a permanent open wound we need to take care of every day, every minute, we can take care of it for some time and then we let it heal, as time is the best medicine and the worst part of it all, we cannot change the past not matter how much we cry, and to make matters worse people who inflicted damage or hurt us are probably living happily ever after, we just need to move on, as everything in this universe is in constant change, nothing stays still, everything moves on, whether we like it or not. And is always for the better, is in our best interest to keep on moving with the pace of this Universe, how much we wish to have the best of everything for as long as we live but that is just not possible it cannot be like that, as we don't know what is in the best interest in the greater plan of God, we ignore what plan he has for us; God had a great plan for Jesus and it was a very difficult one, starting from the moment he came to life when he was born, even though he was the son of God, he came to this world in the worst circumstances, without a home, a cold night, and a short time after he was born, his parents needed to move away quickly and walk 430 miles in rough mountains through two deserts, to save the baby life, at a time when traveling was very tough, nothing was easy very little cloths very little of everything and perhaps and most likely, lack of everything.

And then at the end of his physical life, his most horrible death as if he had been the worst criminal ever existed since humanity existed. When the only thing he did was to bless and to teach. Why understanding this is important to become like a child? Because out of the worse pain the ability to forgive; a virtue? A gift? Is an attitude in the worse circumstances, the same attitude a child has after an offense, why? They have a tender heart a big heart.

Many times when someone push a little we blow up and is not because the circumstance in question was the motive but is more likely a pain from the past if I have an wound open under my cloths and someone comes all of a sudden and push my wound for any reason, I lose my nerves from the pain on the inflicted wound already there and we blame others for hurting us but in reality the wound was always there, and for as long as someone approaches me a certain way my reaction might always be the same, and whomever approach me during this sensitive times would always be feeling guilty for hurting me but in reality is that open wound that is actually pushing people away, and just because we never heal those open wounds, we may manipulate our pain to make others feel guilty too and many times we might have so many sensitive issues we haven't been able to heal, and we inflict pain specially on the person who is next to us and love us dearly because we are living pretending we are normal when in reality if we open our clothes in the soul we are full of open wounds, and how difficult is to live with someone who's pain is not heal is very destructive, we have so much responsibility to heal in order to give the very best of us to others, is only healing when we can love freely, is only healing when our anger dissipates like fog, is only healing when we can really experience the very best of life as we will encounter most situations in a neutral mood, not on an edgy mood ready to strike. I can only imagine how many people have broken apart out of these open wounds we never heal, as soon as someone gets too close to them, we strike with passion and anger, we are unfortunately too complicated but learning to know ourselves is imperative to heal if we get certain feelings due to bad experiences in our past and if we still cry chances are we haven't healed yet and this very circumstance is a motive to turn the pain into a rage inside unconsciously or a depressive behavior and this is the very reason we become so irritable, because pain and anger holding hands is a passive action and reaction, but if we don't learn from children to forget the offenses and especially from Jesus we will be very bitter.

"Right away they extend him over the cross, they stretch his right arm over the right side of the cross, they tight the arm with strength; and one of them put his knee over his sacred chest, another open his hand and a third one put a long and thick nail over his hand, and hit it with an iron hammer. A painful moan came out of Jesus' chest: His blood splashed over the arms of the executioners. I tried to count the hammer strikes but I forgot. The nails were very long a thick head and the head the size of a coin: the nails have three corners; the thickness of a thumb; the point of the nail came out of the other side of the cross. After they nail the right hand of the savior; the executioners realize the left hand was not long enough to reach the left hole of the cross: they tight a rope to his left arm and pull with all their strength until the hand reaches the hole of the cross. This violent dislocation of his arms torment him in such a horrible way: his chest rise and his knees got separated; they kneel again over his body, they tight his arm and bury the second nail on his left hand; the sound of the whining of our Lord could be heard in the middle of the strikes of the hammer. The arms of Jesus were extended horizontally in a way that didn't cover the cross, they were at an angle.

Virgin Mary felt the pain of her son entirely; she was very pale like a dead body, deep painful moans came out of her chest. All the Pharisees would insult her and make fun of her, Mary Magdalene was acting like crazy; she would tear her face and her eyes and cheeks were bleeding.

From the visions of Anne Catherine Emmerich (1774-1824)

We don't understand what kind of pain our good Lord experienced throughout the ordeal of the last hours of his life but even with all the torture and pain, he was able to ask God for their forgiveness, just to show us we could do the same, asking God to forgive our offenders is the beginning in the process of healing we don't necessarily have to let go right away but asking God to forgive our offenders is the beginning, with time and constant prayer, one day at a time, eventually, our love to the creator will take over, and all of our pain in our heart will heal, huge lesson indeed, We simply have not excuse.

> Then Peter came to Jesus and asked, "Lord, how many times shall I forgive my brother who sins against me? Up to seven times?" Jesus answered, "I tell you, not just seven times, but seventy-seven times!... *Matthew 18:21*

And this is what little children do, they just forgive and move on, not wonder Jesus said we most become like children to get in the kingdom of heaven, and that is the same thing with many other good things we left behind along the road as were growing, thinking we don't have to carry them in our adult luggage like the ability to simply believe, when we tell our children a story they are mesmerize with everything we tell them and they believe, as we grow we need proof or we simply don't believe, everything has to have a reason and a scientific explanation, but we are the ones who created science to find a reason for everything that surround us, because we find an infinite intelligence able to engineer and create everything just too simple, and when we discover a clue and do little investigation and find the reasoning we simply deduce everything has a reason and a scientific proof and we go on, until one day we find the door closed on our investigation, we can't go forward not more, then we start creating theories making all sorts of assumptions because believing other than science is just too foolish, but many prophets in the scripture tell us, what happened when we turn away from God and Paul the apostle tell us:

> *For the message of the cross is foolishness to those who are perishing, but to us who are being saved it is the power of God. For it is written: "I will destroy the wisdom of the wise; the intelligence of the intelligent I will frustrate."...*
> *Where is the wise man? Where is the scribe? Where is the philosopher of this age? Has not God made foolish the wisdom of the world? For since in the wisdom of God, the*

> *world through its wisdom did not know Him, God was*
> *pleased through the foolishness of what was preached to save*
> *those who believe.*
>
> *Jews demand signs and Greeks search for wisdom, but*
> *we preach Christ crucified, a stumbling block to Jews and*
> *foolishness to Gentiles, but to those who are called, both Jews*
> *and Greeks, Christ the power of God and the wisdom of God.*
> *Corinthians 1:18,24*

We need to believe, to enter in the kingdom of heaven, because if we don't, during the time of our short existence, we will find at the last moments of death how wrong and mistaken we have been, but it would already be too late, as the key to faith, is "to believe", if there was a high-speed highway and the bridge fell on the other side of a mountain, into an abyss, and someone miraculously survives the accident and comes back and flags everybody down to turn around to stop, and head another way, many drivers would see his clothes all torn apart and would think he is crazy and just keep going, many others would stop hear what he has to say but proceed slowly even if he tells them not to do that, as they would not be able to stop once they are on the other side of the hill but they don't believe either, but a few would believe and turn around, the scripture in a way is like that, is a warning and is flashing like a traffic signal, at some point in our life and one way or another it will come in front of our eyes, perhaps in subliminal messages and many of us would just not believe, maybe written in the back of a truck or something we read and that particular phrase is stock in our mind pointing us in that direction, many of us would think about it a little but keep on going not problem, some others would stop on their tracks, they would believe and turn around, something like this happen to me and I think the timing is also the perfect time just like a fruit when is ripe, there is a time for everything if this had happened early in my life perhaps I would just keep on going like a freight train, and many times we need to grow some more to acknowledge the voice of the Lord calling, this is why we can't get frustrated when some people reject the message and think we are crazy, they are simply not ready yet, like the old say "we can bring the horse to the river but we can't make it drink" there is no reason to get angry is an opportunity to exercise patience and to pray for the non-believers or for the ones that believe but pretend he doesn't know what they do, our prayers should never be selfish all about us, we have the obligation to pray for so much need around us and the whole world, remember the roman soldier who asks Jesus to heal his servant, whom his master value highly and Jesus heal him, this is the power of intersection when you pray for others, maybe the servant didn't deserve to be healed but because the roman ask with faith Jesus heal him, with our prayers we may help heal the spirit of many.

I know all of us get opportunities to stop many times before we fall in to the abyss and I think God is so merciful that many who live their lives as if there was not tomorrow, doing whatever their senses guide them to, not conscious at all, this people may get, many times a longer life just to give them plenty of the opportunity to stop and turn around and find the way, if you ever wonder why do bad people many times live so many years is just the mercy of God, when his apostle Thomas didn't believe because he didn't see Jesus resurrected with his own eyes he told the other apostles he have to touch him to believe, he have to see him to believe, this same attitude is very familiar to all of us, even most of us perhaps at some point we have behave just like Thomas, I hope we change in to truthful believers and with the grace of God get closer to him, and also help others along the way, but as with all the other good qualities of a children, believing is a gift, one we must own to become like the children. Many times I see children running and laughing so much and I feel joy because with so little they have so much fun with so little they make an ordinary day in to an extraordinary and their happiness is contagious, many adults get irritated just to hear them laugh and play around but to me is like slapping a butterfly, the joy of seen a butterfly with those beautiful colors tossing around in the air and joyful stopping everywhere then a slap to kill the beauty, it feels the same as during this times especially now, many kids this days live like zombies in a virtual world, this kind of kid is a handicap as the real world of socializing with other kids is alien to many of them they rather be virtual where they can hide in a corner from the world, how damaging and terrible is that, we need more children laughter more children playing, and it has always been through many centuries the best way to learn to socialize, it is however during this times very difficult, as we now have a culture of isolating kids in their virtual world. This joy so natural in children is part of the package we need, the ability to laugh, to enjoy the moment without worries, and just be happy even in the worst circumstances, a survivor of the concentration camps of WWII when he was a prisoner he learns that the ability to survive was not reserved for the strong, the smart, but to the ones who chose to, and put their minds to survive even besides the worse possible circumstances, it was a mental choice to keep a feeling of optimism even when everything is lost, those who lost hope were death. Like that is our choice to enjoy the moment, is our choice to be happy, is our choice to live in the present, and is our choice to believe in God and his promises.

"Jesus said to him because you have seen me, you have believed; blessed are those who have not seen, and yet have believed." (John 20:29). If we hit a little kid, he might run and hide, in fear, he would be scare, he can't defend himself and we are certain he won't come back to hurt us, because that is how children are, vulnerable they would cry and fall sleep and tomorrow is just another fresh new day, perhaps the next day he is a little quiet but a little play, a tickle, a funny joke and he is good to go, another thing we need to learn from the children behavior is the ability to suppress the anger and channel this energy into their imagination, they walk away from what just happen and don't focus their attention to that anymore, change their attention to anything else, they slowly move on to something else and concentrate their senses to play, to their imagination, to their day dreams, or to simply fall sleep, during their painful moments they burst in to tears, after that probably fall sleep, and wake up fresh; when we as adults get hurt, a lot of us, our first reaction is to react and use that anger to try to hurt our offender, because otherwise we would be consider fools according to our own adult judgment, and our always first adviser "pride", we start to recreate everything over in our minds over and over, many times, we might play this picture to imagine, how we could hurt the offender or say the exact words to show we are strong, what we would had done differently to adjust the scenery to whatever make us feel better and this could go on and on, perhaps many years, but our growing desire to revenge to hurt and many times we try to do justice immediately as soon as we get hurt, we just have this urge to get back, maybe we obey to a natural instinct, or maybe we just too angry to think, and we feel is the right thing to do, to just get back and become violent and aggressive;

this is another moment when we are tested and have the ability to turn around and pray is just a hard to learn discipline, especially if we know we have a short spark a hard temper, if we follow our desire to hurt back the offender and go on with our negative actions, somehow we never feel right, deep inside there is an emptiness a pain, a sense of something is not right, maybe some regret and this is our conscious reprehending our actions, and if we don't feel anything it only shows how corrupt we have become, how difficult is to become a child during this testing period and this might continuously happen over and over until we learn, as repetition usually happens with all the other many situations we encounter in our life, they are constant test over and over, until our weakness is strengthen and we react differently and eventually, this situations, all of a sudden disappear, we for certain cannot do it alone is probably beyond our strength, it is for that matter necessary to pray and trust, learn from the scripture to realize how powerful God and his justice reaches all the corners of the universe, how he takes care of the offense, read(Jeremiah 17: 9-10). And for the offender, our creator sees straight up to our heart, read (1 Samuel 16:7) a contrite heart is necessary as God sees right through, and how sometimes he took justice on the second generation or the third, it is a mystery as to how our creator takes justice, but he is not only merciful he is also just; this, for instance, becomes, a great deal of faith, to know when we let our creator deal with our battles we don't need to fight them, when we do this we need a lot of prayers. If we get an instance where something happened unexpectedly and we react to an offender in the same way and add more wood to the raging fire, our learning and discipline are still very poor, our faith is weak, no reason to get discouraged, understand pray and try to do the right thing again until we achieve results; is in the fire where the real gold is tested, how could we endure and survive this battles? And have the strength courage to remain in silence or walk away? The answer is in two parts one is we have to be prepared for situations like this how? When we do a great deal of praying and live thinking constantly in our first love, Jesus; our soul starts to calm down and live at peace and if a situation emerges we are prepared with a shield to take on the offense with more strength to handle harsh situations, and the second is to pray for the offender for their wellbeing and for us to get covered with meekness, to have the courage to live with the embarrassment, to have been humiliated and hurt even when we can get back and hurt, this is exactly what Jesus did with the exception, he was also loving his offenders, but Jesus was perfect we can follow his steps and hope prayer gets the best of our selves. Don't do what our emotions force us to, discipline with prayer is the key; just like a rich man can let lose all his perversions and to whatever comes in his mind but he doesn't, instead, he does good deeds, he is well seen, to the eyes of our creator, the same way when we don't react to our anger in that way, our instinct and rage is contained like a dog with rabies in a cage when we do this, we are giving fruits to our faith, it's not easy but is possible even when we think we have the worst temper, but is a path where we need assistance from our creator, we need to start reading the scripture to understand how our creator deals with many of the situations in the lives of many men who had direct interaction with God, the scripture would make us stronger when we have to face these real-life battles, and help us to trust God, to respect life, to transform us into a new man, even if those who know you, would criticize you, and judge you, the old you is slowly fading away, just rest in the hands of Jesus, he is the craftsman and can mold us into a new pot, How much we need to learn from children! We must become like children to get into the kingdoms of heaven.

A child can see things with innocence and not awake evil instincts like adults, when King David saw Bathsheba the wife of Uriah, taking a shower in his garden he was tempted, he lay with her, and was displeased by the Lord. When Eva was tempt with the delicious fruit, she saw the tree and realize it was good for food and that it was a delight to the eyes, she believe the serpent, she took of its fruit and ate, and displeased the Lord, how difficult is to be like a child, and have a pure and clean heart, it is a challenge but this is what we should strive for, most times this small decision we made when tempted has huge consequences I often call this the five minutes of stupidity we all have those at some point in our life, many people for five minutes of stupidity lost their lives, lost their family or end up in jail or worse like in the case of Eva when she had her five minutes the consequences up to this day are echoing the pain generation after generation, during temptation is easy to fail when our association with the Lord is remote, the closer we get to God the more chances we have of success is just the consequence, just like when we work out we get stronger the same way when we become closer to God we pray, we fast, we exercise the spirit in silence and read the gospels we get stronger and better prepared for this five minute of terrible battles those five minutes and a life of remorse, I often see people in the news who had a life time of normality and five minutes that put them in the spot light, I can't help not to feel pain, if we could be stronger and make better decisions each and every moment, we cannot have positive results simple with our own strength, we might never have it, because we are naturally weak, this is why if you can change your heart and feed your spirit is in your own benefit as you just never know when those five minutes would come they often come when we are just more vulnerable or when we feel so secure of our strength, let's be like sheep but wise like serpents is in the gospel, find the little child we lost but keep your adulthood for sagacity.

One day I had a test, as my temper has always been bad, and after I started to try to walk on track and decided to change, it happen, on this day I was involved in a situation of violence not on my part but I was attacked, I remember I was so calm inside and didn't feel nothing at all, not emotions inside, my only goal was to contain the attacker, finally I was able to force him to the ground, I received a hit on my head with a car club (a steering wheel lock device) while we struggle, and I was bleeding, but felt no pain, I pin him down and I was in a situation where I could hurt him with my fists, if I wanted to, as I had his arms lock under my knees, I just couldn't as all this learning audiobooks, the scripture and many spiritual books were already working and constantly bouncing on my head, I was slowly acquiring peace inside, my spirit was calm, I just couldn't and all I did, was to hold him there until police arrived, when one officer approach me and told me, he got you pretty good ah! Nodding negatively, I felt humiliated as I knew I could had hurt him so bad as other times in my past of my violent rages, my pride was hurt and I wish, for a moment I hadn't change, but I did, and eventually, I understood it was a test, a part of my past that came to haunt me, as inside of me, I knew I change, but there comes the day when we will be tested; as I move on with my life later on, I acquire a dog, we name her Roxy, she was adorable but she always had the tendency to chew on anything that comes her way, every time you turn around there was some destruction, this cause me a lot of anger, as many times the things she chew on, were expensive and when you struggle to make a dollar it hurts even more, we bought a wicker outdoor set, within a week she had partially destroyed the table and some of the other chairs, this always cause me to irritate myself and loose it, I would hit her sometimes, some others I just ignore it, and later on she would look at me with her sorry huge eyes and you had no option but love her more, hoping love would change her, this behavior continue on, one time after the other, maybe once a month or twice, but it would really make me hit the ceiling, when she rip something then sometimes I loose it, I felt terrible, it was a pattern, how can I think and believe I have changed, and still have this kind of behavior this was really troubling me, until the last time it happen I went on a prayer, I heard a voice inside telling me something, it chill my bones, this is how it happened.

That day I leash her to the frame of my boat, as we have a partial fence and I cannot let her loose unless I'm outside, afraid she might disturb and annoy the neighbors, like she had done before, I figure she would be ok until we come back from going somewhere that day, I scope the scene and thought to myself she is going to be ok, there is nothing she could chew, when we came back she somehow reach the cover of my boat and rip it, I remember I made some sacrifice this past summer to buy the cover, I lost it, again, and the whole ordeal started again, after everything was done, I went inside the house and later I started praying and meditating about this situation when somewhere inside my conscious I hear this voice telling me this; that is exactly, what you did to me, and I never hit you, you treat me like that over and over you rip me and destroyed me, one time after the other and I never hit you, I had compassion on you and waited for you to change and this is how most people treat me and I'm still waiting on them, I don't hit them, somehow this words appear in my head, I felt the need to go on my knees and pray for forgiveness, and cried.

So you see God is always interacting and teaching us, in ways we could not figure out, we need to be open to those voices in the silence of our meditations to hear, if there is something we need to fix in order to move on to the next lesson, I know for certain now, not matter what happen, I would not have the heart to hit Roxy is been a couple of years now. How great is the amount of learning in order to be a little perfect each day before God.

The innocence of thinking good about everybody another great quality of children, how often we criticize and judge people, how often we talk about others in a bad way, when they are not even there to defend themselves, how many times have we fall in to this trap? When we hear others in a group, talk about someone and incredibly we fall in to the spider web of words just adding to the judgment everyone is doing, how many times in our interactions and conversations with other people is about our peers, coworkers, friends, and I don't mean good conversations where we admire and talk good about others, is the bad judgment we're doing and the criticism we're doing, this is where we fall short from greatness as we cannot imagine or walk on other people shoes to see why they did what they did, perhaps we would have done the same thing or worst, we just don't know.

We are all on the same field playing the game, maybe today we didn't run, maybe today we catch all those balls, maybe today we score but that doesn't mean tomorrow we would have the same circumstances and the same game, as quickly as the day comes, we may have different players and different fields just as much as we would like to think, "we today have the perfect game, the perfect life" we are not immune to tragedy, to heartbreaking, to deceit, to pain, that is a fact, and we can easily become the main characters of a new soap opera in real life; so where our weakness to judge, and criticize so easily come from? Is just in our nature that tends to do it, plus we learn from our role models as with a great percentage of our rights thoughts and wrong thoughts, our egos are boosted to think we would have done differently and better, this is probably far from the truth.

Children of shortage don't judge and criticize, they are ready to play, to smile, to enjoy, they don't see our dirty clothes or shiny shoes, they don't care if we are black or white, is just a genuine little guy who would talk, play and enjoy if you interact with him, later on, he would simply forget you, as he could get entertain with anything else and if they see tears in your eyes they would feel empathy if they see a smile they would smile back; no wonder our creator said we should become like children if we want to get in the kingdom of heaven.

How difficult is it to be more like children, many times we should think for a moment when we encounter certain circumstances, what Jesus would do in this situation? If we ask this question, we might very well have a lot of problems with the answer, because is a difficult answer, we know the things Jesus would have done in many situations we have every day, they are, sometimes hard things to do, like humiliate yourself by holding your mouth when you know you can answer back, like not punching back when someone does, like forgive the most horrible things that we have endure due to the evil of others, like not getting angry easy, it is extremely hard but is very well possible if we keep a constant prayer, we are like clay, we could be mold, not matter if we think our heart is like a hard cold iron, even if we feel tough like rocks, we can change and start feeling lighter and better, or when we are financially broke and we feel we deserve a lot more but just don't have it yet, and we ask the question, it might be a tough answer, we may take the opportunity to glorify God when we offer him our sufferings and struggles and weakness is at least a good way to start getting back up.

FAITH IS JUST
A DECISION

If we feel down for our situation, we might ask why someone has financial freedom and successful life. The question alone is negative as it may place us in a measure made by men, we measure success not the way God do, for some reason we want it all, to fill a void that has not limits, even if we own the whole planet the time will come when we would want the moon, and we would be the same if we have it, or not, is the essence inside where we have to work to find content and be at peace; we could glorify and honor God in the place where we are, in the place where we are born, in the circumstances we are at, we should strive for the best but when we are experiencing pain, suffering and illness is a great opportunity to glorify God, as pain and suffering when is offer as a sacrifice for our mistakes, and for the entire world, it creates a healing process, and the bitter pain slowly could fade, many times we believe when we have everything, our health, financial stability, when everything goes well we could praise God much better, and is probably true but is during those good times we become forgetful, we could praise our creator in any circumstance and for certain when we are carrying the heavy burden of a cross, with a lot of pain just like Jesus did, and we offer this pain in sacrifice, we can definitely be certain our connection to heaven would be more strong, why I'm so certain of this, because all of his disciples suffer and die martyrs except for John and when they did they were content, because their faith was blind, they knew the promise was certain, why is suffering a common denominator of the most faithful is our Lord decision, all I'm saying is don't get discourage when you suffer in any way, don't lose your faith, stay calm as much as possible and put your thoughts in what you have, if you really look up close is always a lot, if we work the spirit we would be content if we have and the same way if we don't, content does not mean to be conformist, content is to be a peace while we work on our goals, in exercising the spirit is when we could make permanent change, I insist on change because we all need it, I know for personal experience is a priority the sooner we start the less mistakes we might prevent, in my words is like destroying the animal inside to become the human we all need to be, like Jesus said we need to be born again and if we put it in perspective this is why the world is so wild there is more animal in the humanity than there is a true human.

> Now I rejoice in what I am suffering for you, and I fill
> up in my flesh what is still lacking in regard to Christ's
> afflictions, for the sake of his body, which is the church.
> Colossians 1:24

Not in my life time I ever thought, I would change so many things I had, they were many times I felt, I would die a certain way because that is who I am, and if people didn't like it too bad, if this phrase sounds familiar, I encourage you to invite Jesus and his teachings in to your life as well as all the other scriptures in the Bible, spiritual, motivational books; now a days in a world so self-sufficient, a world where God is almost like a myth, a world with so cold hearted men and women, a world that never think about our creator, we just simply forgot him, we don't make him part of our everyday life, if Jesus was our cell-phone, how much better we would be, how many troubles we would have avoided, how much peace we would have; in the scripture every time the Israelites forgot about their savior and creator and worship other Gods they would suffer either by becoming slaves, they would get tyrants for kings, constant wars, constant pain, hunger, destruction, drought, and many other bad things and is all because is in suffering when we go back and bend our knees, is only when we face tragedy, we realize how weak and small we really are, we are unable to make rain, to make the fields grow healthy crop, we are unable to stop all adversity's in our life, we depend on the Sun, the moon, the water, the fertile ground, or when we are sick, we find out how weak we really are, there is not enough money and weapons in the world to save us, we just don't have any control or power just as much as we would like to think, does this many sufferings today have a relation with our distance from God? Where do we put our heart and trust? If we do it in another man we would certainly die, if we put it in our money, we are blind and egocentric, if we put it in our weapons we are fools, but if we trust in God we would never be disappointed. Just as in the ancient times when the Israelites, walk away from God, destruction and tragedy came into their life's we are so much due for so much pain, we are sadly blind, stubborn, cold-hearted, ignorant, naive, and complete fools as we have always been over and over we keep doing the same mistakes to ourselves, in our homes, to our families, in the groups we belong, in society and our countries, we think many things in the world are ok while it doesn't interfere in my life, for example, if someone

Abort a baby is ok, is her life and her body, is the freedom we say, not the right time, is a mistake; we don't realize evil utilize our freedom as a tool. Right is right, wrong is wrong there is not middle there is not bargaining we accommodate our laws to our comfort to our human ideals of perfection, "thou shall not kill" is one of the commandments, when we legalize abortion not matter how much we think we love God, we are just been hypocrites, we vote for a yes on killing babies and then on Saturday or Sunday we go to church and do a great deal of breast beating, we support the idea because whatever we want to think and justified the idea however we want, is meaningless, it just goes against God, is that simple, if we ever did support it, if we ever vote for a yes, I hope God could touch your heart when you see a child who had the opportunity to live and think about all the millions who never had a chance; if we ever have part on it, by paying to do an abortion, by doing it, by participating; I got news for you, we have our hands with blood, we most certainly have a lot to explain when we come face to face to the divine tribunal, no question about it, God is merciful but he is very just, as well, I know for certain nothing will change on the contrary I got the feeling is here to stay, but we should teach our children, help them understand the divine laws should be imprinted in our heads, and if we had part in this irreversible evil we most repent and have a contrite heart before we leave this world. I didn't see it always the way I do today, this has, like many things in my life been haunting me too, I became part of this terrible act, as I somehow accept to do it, even against my will, but I even pay for it, now I carry this heavy burden for the rest of my life, if I only knew back then, what I know now, there are no words to describe this pain especially when you have kids you love with all of your heart, sometimes when I see them, I wonder what would that baby that I didn't give a chance to live, look like, whom would he ever become, what if my mother would have prevented my birth? Taking away the opportunity to be here and not been able to accomplish what I came for, just because she was scared, just because she felt she couldn't face the world, or just because as a baby, I would have been an obstacle in her life, how selfish and a coward would she have been when at the end of the day the Lord rewards you if you don't interfere with our creator plan, and since God is so just, he would probably have a way to recriminate our wrongdoing.

Yes I was a coward, a selfish, egocentric fool, and I pray for mercy as I kill my baby too, and there is nothing I could do to amend that, I regret all of it but there is no fixing I just pray for forgiveness, I always pray for many soon to be mothers and fathers, to have the courage to go on, as their courage would be rewarded by our creator sooner or later, and the joy a little human can bring, is beyond measure, don't hesitate, pray for guidance as our Lord is a God of life! is a creator, is an architect of life, for life and to life. There is only one who is against life and is not even worth mentioning the name here, as he has been responsible for all evil in all of human history, and is so jealous because we are sons and daughters of God and he is just a creature with no relationship, not for one moment think you are pleasing God if you go against life. Going forward with the plan our creator has set for an unborn baby is participating with his great master plan, going against is destroying our lives and many other lives this baby would have one day touch. But as with everything else we do, we don't consider God law, and we disrupt natural laws, this may sound antiquated, radical to today's mentality but nowadays we come up with any logic to explain the wrong in the name of freedom, this may be harsh words but the early Christians were not afraid to openly object to any wrongdoing because they believe, we read the Gospel and forget to do what Jesus apostles did after Jesus resurrected they went around the world teaching, we just don't teach anymore, we are all called to teach the Gospel, we should take action not just church on the weekend and that is all we need, we start with, our kids, our close family members, our friends, nowadays we are ashamed to do it, Jesus would also be ashamed of us too, read (Luke 9:26) We use our mouth for everything, and we know our words have power, when we have a business we brag about it, when we have a beautiful home we do the same, we brag about our kids, our vacation, but we don't dare to brag about your powerful God, maybe is because we are not proud of him and not thoroughly convince of his existence. This bring me another interesting topic that many always question and it is important, why do we have the certainty and why do we trust believe and have faith in Jesus, because many of us have a tendency to think everything is the same but it is not, there was a men who cut history in half this is how important this men was we are two thousand something since he was born and in the year zero history was divided forever.

If all of the religions were created by men then it would be too arrogant to say Christianity is the right path to heaven, but what if one of them was not created by men it was a path set from our creator, Jesus came to the world and he proclaimed he was God, he made signs, not one in the history of men kind could do, convert several jars full of hundred litters of water in to the best wine, multiply bread and fish to feed five thousand people when he only had very few, in front of thousands, he made this miracle twice, he cure the sick, he gave sight to many blind people, he cure people immediately of leper, he walked on water, he resuscitate death people, he was resuscitated after his crucifixion, and appear to hundreds of people in different occasions after his death sending his followers to teach the nations what he taught them, he made hundreds of signs no man could ever do, and he claim he was the son of God, therefore his divinity, he is recorded in history as a truthful character, his teaching is the truth, the way, the life, those who believe and follow his teaching with the heart would be saved, Jesus said everything would pass but my word would never pass, if we are not moved by all his miracles and teachings where the main and only idea is pure and genuine love, and love for others how much different this world would be if all of us believe in his message and lived by his teachings from the heart where a genuine change in the heart would really make us believers and followers, how much different the world would be, if we love,

113

if we really forgive, if we have faith, if we trust. We could one day be living at peace with love, with no crooked intentions to hurt others, and to judge others, to help more, to be sympathetic and feel pain for the injustice, to feel shame for our wrongdoing. Why are we so stubborn? Is it because we are in love with the illusion this world offer, in the form of pleasure, money, and material things, all of these are meant to disguise what the truth is, and is not a bad thing to have all of these, the problem begins when we forget who all of this things come from, who is above, the problem is what these things mean to us if they become more important sometimes even more important than our own life, there is no difference between worshiping other Gods or making everything else more important in our lives, is just the same we worship our cars, our cellphones, our homes, our pleasures, our bodies, our money so you see we do have a lot of Gods, so what makes us different from the Israelites in the times of the kings or the judges or when they were in the desert and forgot their creator, there is no difference now and then, perhaps different clothes, But what do we expect from our creator? If we read during the times of the book of judges and on the forty years in the desert when the people of Israel just complaint over and over they didn't recognize they just have been saved from the Egyptians in the most formidable and amazing way, they pretended nothing happen, how much pain our merciful and loveable God endure, how much sadness an patience for a lovable God, not been recognized as your savior and creator even when they saw what he did, there is not difference now when Jesus was hung on a cross to pay for all our sins and besides all of his signs, miracles and his works and his word, everything is still the same way, his word is ignored, we just complaint over and over, pray only in a selfish way only asking and asking and never recognizing, acknowledging his mercy and all of his love for human kind, the sacrifice he made for us in the cross, even when all he did was good deeds, we are not worth been saved, and yet our creator has faith for some estrange reason in human kind, because we are the same people over and over and over, doing the same mistakes generation after generation. I am amazed at how much love and how much patience our creator has, it is just amazing, probably angels can't even understand his love and mercy for humanity, and he tries and tries over and over but we just don't understand, we don't comprehend it. we are just too comfortable, we are just too lazy, we are just too blind to see, to hear, and even when we read, we don't understand our life is just too short, our time is just so little, but yet we spend it like if we are eternal, we say and do things like if we would never have to explain every single word we said, or all of the things we do, one day after this life we will if we love to talk we must refrain, don't talk to talk when we do it should be productive and positive. We are immersed in our little world, or we are immersed in the world of technology where we forgot our reality and our purpose all of these distractions are meant to separate us from God, we could use them to learn, to promote, to teach, but we use them just to kill time, to play meaningless games or read nonsense. Going back to basics and make our own family a small church, start simply as the first Christians did, their life's were evolving around for Jesus, with Jesus, and in Jesus, if we do this our environments everywhere would change even if we see the worst of the circumstances and the situations are terrible, as Jesus works come slowly, start with yourself, then bring your family and whomever you come in contact with, show your pride

To be the son of God as we have the honor to be, don't forget the good, will always be attacked.

Our kids are always on their electronic devices they are like empty containers and empty remain, until one day someone fills them up with lots of bad information and the wrong information just because you didn't do your job you procrastinate with your most precious possession, and now is too late someone already fills up their heads and everything you want to pour in is already spilling, how terrible, what are we doing, why so much laziness? Why so much lack of interest, when are we going to learn? I know is the enemy works everywhere, we have warnings, but we neglect to see them just like when we driving and the gas needle goes on red, we may say I know I can go just a little more, we wait to the next day to talk, then the next day never comes until is already too late.

Why when we have the power to inspire our little ones and others don't take the time and effort to do it, why is so hard to take the first step? Why we feel will have them tomorrow and the next day or the next one, is an everyday process is a small seed in the heart of the ones we care about, we must plant and water every day.

How can we learn if no one teaches anymore? The Ethiopian eunuch on the scripture acknowledges he didn't understand the scripture as he was

115

reading when he was returning home, he was humble enough to realize he did not understand and Philip was brought in by the Holy Spirit to teach him, as when the student is ready the master would appear. We must be ready and willing to take steps toward a better life, if you wonder, is there something better for me even besides all of my circumstances? The answer is yes, there is, always going to be yes, but everything starts from inside where the darkness has taken place and has covered all or a big portion of our life, it could start with just one simple click, or when we walk away from all those everyday things we are obsessed with, one-click in a direction to inspirational audio or an application to another job, it could start in the classifies adds with an opportunity, or with a book a course on something we could learn new or a talk with someone who could inspire you.

When the Ethiopian eunuch return home he probably set the base for the Christian church in his country it was part of God plan to have him converted and bring the word of Jesus in Ethiopia, we would never know how he started and how he did it but one thing is certain God was working with him, right next to him, to bring the word of God to his people, but for all this things to happen he was reading the scripture he was working the ground for when the seed come, the soil would be fertile, he was doing something to allow the works of God to happen to become something; if we don't work the soil, find the tools, remove the weed, and get the ground ready, we could not expect to get a harvest of any kind, even just removing weed is a lot of work, a great amount of times we see the weed and just decide to leave it there, because the amount of work is required to get rid of it, how many of us have so much weed, and we are used to live with it, each of us in moments of silence and meditation should look deep inside and determine what is weed in our life?, and what is preventing a good seed to be planted in our heart, there is one truth we all agree and it is the fact everything in life is work, everything moves and nothing in this planet is not subject to change, as for the creatures of God he has a plan a task and a mission with specific instructions, as for us since we are sons and daughters of God, we have the liberty to do as wish and just like the prodigal son in the scripture, read(*Luke 15:11-32)*, waste all of our life doing what we think is correct, what we think is right, what we believe is according to our perception of things and our reality, we have a very limited vision of the road ahead, and very limited vision of the whole picture and plan, one way to start is never to trust in yourself, never trust to have the power to overcome hurdles by yourself, never trust to have the knowledge to walk the entire path by yourself, if you rely on your intelligence, on your muscles, on your money, and your weapons, we are in for a fight we will fail, unless that, which you set to do becomes successful by yourself is because is in God greatest plan to be that way, for a purpose, but not by your talent and ability; God use Nebuchadnezzar to do a lot of his work, he was not a Jew he was just a powerful king and he didn't know he was in fact working for the Lord, this is why sometimes even if we are far from the truth and our plans come together, perhaps it is in his plan to be this way.

Nebuchadnezzar was a very powerful king in ancient times who was used by God to accomplish the plans he had for him, although Nebuchadnezzar was like every human on earth, his ego made him believe he was there by his means,

> You, O king, are a king of kings. For the God of heaven has given you a kingdom, power, strength, and glory; and wherever the children of men dwell, or the beasts of the field and the birds of the heaven, He has given them into your hand, and has made you ruler over them all—you are this head of gold. (Daniel 2-37-38)

Nothing good we believe we do or accomplish is from our work, is part of the plan, don't ever trust just in yourself to fight your battles, to climb the uphill path, to work for a dream, to achieve something, ask in a humble way for God help, ask for the wisdom and the knowledge to move on, at everything you set your mind to, if it is meant to be it will happen, even the son of God, Jesus in the prayer of Gethsemane said:

> *"My Father, if possible, let this cup pass from me; nevertheless, not as I will, but as you will"(Matthew 26-39)*

It is to show us the will of the Father overcomes our own will, and not always is going to be as we wish, not always as we want, because what comes next is something bigger something better, Jesus drinks the bitter cup to teach us a lesson we don't like, a lesson where things go in the opposite direction of our plans and dreams, and yes we are free but we have a purpose, a plan, a reason, either we sit down and do nothing, we do things but we do them all wrong, or we work with the help of God and accepting his will, while we fight to accomplish our dreams, we might not get where we wanted but when we accept the will of the Father we can be certain is for a better purpose for a better plan.

In my personal experience I always did things but I trusted myself and did it all wrong if I ever score was because it was in the greatest plan of the creator to be that way, even those who don't believe in God have their lives directed by him, and it's presented as the author of their existence, in many ways, to see if either by touching and sensing, or by admiring the amazing nature, or by analogy, by the unexplained mysteries the reason can never understand, they can experience his presence and maybe they can find it or see it nor less understand it.

Science can make our life so much easier, more comfortable, it could help us travel, learn, heal and in general give us a better life, but the basic question where we come from? How do we come to exist? Science could never have an answer to because the answer is incomprehensible for science, but for us people of faith the answer is simple as we are aware of our nature and everything in existence; we can't argue, we just believe as we see the miracles in our everyday life, we are blessed because we believe as Jesus promises to his disciples,

"Blessed are those who believe without seeing" John 20-29 as of today, I walk slowly in my life but I have the certainty the hand of God is working in my life, and is an amazing feeling to know the direction was traced by the infinite intelligence of the above, accept what we can't change, change what we can if it is for something better, and wait for his promise, remember when we were kids and we played at falling backward knowing the person behind you, would catch you, that is the feeling I walk nowadays, is the knowledge my creator is waiting for me when I fall back to catch me every single time, nowadays whatever comes my way I simply keep silence to the problems that arise every day with the assurance my Lord is behind every time, nowadays I understand a leaf on a tree falls because that was my creator will, I keep fighting for my dreams, I keep dreaming, I keep learning, I keep moving forward, but I know when my feet stagger, he is there to comfort me, and to give me strength, for as long as I keep moving forward and live my life according to his teachings, I know he is next to me, this trust is a gift comes from above it is given slowly with prayer, as the relationship grows, I understand is not easy, to trust but it's much better than relying on your own, because of our human nature we are just simply full of limitations, and mistakes are part of our nature.

"Behold, I lay in Zion a chief cornerstone, elect, precious, And he who believes on Him will by no means be put to shame." 1 Peter 2:6

Science on the other hand concerning what they don't understand fills the scientific with uncertainty and frustration, as the many mysteries of life are a puzzle, but for us, is perhaps not essential to know the how because knowing why is the same way our Lord see it, for Love.

Peter spend three years of his life with Jesus he was a good friend, learn directly from the son of God, he ate with him, he was witness to countless miracles, he witness Jesus walk on water, resuscitate the dead, multiply the fish, and bread to feed thousands, he acknowledges Jesus is the Messiah and yet Peter fail to trust Jesus in the last day he denied he knew him, he was afraid, he fears for his life, he was very human, he was just weak and he knew him, he certainly loves him, but he was just weak, too afraid to trust, for the rest of us who never witness in those terms all the miracles of God who never learn directly from him and love him the way Peter did, how much harder it is to trust? How much easier it is to deny him? How much harder it is to love him? How much weaker we are, especially when we don't have firsthand memories?

Jesus knows and prevented it would be a lot more difficult for our future generations to believe, to trust, to love, that's why in the cross he has his arms wide open as a symbol to let everyone know he welcome all of us without judging, just like he help the adultery woman:

Then Jesus straightened up and asked her, "Woman, where are your accusers? Has no one condemned you?" "No one, Lord." she answered. "Then neither do I condemn you." Jesus declared. "Now go and sin no more."...(John 8:10-11)

This is what all of us can expect when we come straight to him, his arms wide open and because we are much more difficult to convince since we were not first account witness in Jesus life, his mercy is immense, fathomless, we could deny he is our savior many times and yet when we come back his arms are still wide open, this kind of mercy is just possible to God as he understands our blindness, our stubbornness, our ignorance, our cold hard, our complete misery since we are unable to do anything without his direct or indirect help, the way he looks at us is the same way we look at a baby when he is starting to walk and his steps are clumsy and silly, he sees how we stumble and get a tantrum and cry, he just loves us in a way, not one in this world can, and I have my share of blindness too as there was a time in my life I deny God existence when I was a teenager and I started reading Greek philosophy and more and finally came to the conclusion Everything in existence has a logical reason for everything to exist as if it doesn't have a proven logical explanation and evidence then is probably not true and is probably pure fiction.

I spend some time just feeding my arguments to prove I was right, how I came back to my senses I don't remember it was probably God mercy that touch my heart because I remember the day I change my point of view something inside was feeling warm in the emptiness and cold of my soul, I don't know, and the truth is, I knew very little next to nothing in regards of the word of Jesus even when I learn a few prayers as a kid and assisted to church; what happens with the word of God and Christianity is the same thing we as parents do when we send our kids to school, we expect the teachers would properly raise and help our children, and eventually they would become good kids, literally speaking but it is actually not truth, our teachers compliment and many times polish good kids to make them better, but the main job in regards of their main values, good manners, respect, good examples and ideas about life in general and more importantly their character and behavior, and many other important things for their healthy growth comes from home, the same thing apply to the word of Jesus it is something our parents have to teach and more importantly live every moment by example, and my family was a good family but not very knowledgeable in regards of what it really meant to follow his teachings, a normal family would give you a lot of slack and cut loose your "leash" to do trial and error, and think almost everything is ok, and that is a very thin line between good and bad, where everything is cover with a touch of paint and a little make up, and that way it could be good, this is very dangerous territory as we are opening the door to anything and everything, like if we are used to talk with profanity and our kids listen they think is normal and we think well, I'm a good guy the only thing I do is I use a bad word here and there and or maybe all the time, we are just touching up paint, a bad behavior and a wrong way of thinking because for every word we will be accountable:

> But I tell you that men will give an account on the
> Day of Judgment for every careless word they have spoken.
> Matthew 12-36

Or when we drink alcohol and lose control but we justify it by thinking, well I'm a good hard-working family man, the only thing I do is get drunk socially and not very often, again just justifying our wrong doing:

> "Wine is a mocker, strong drink a brawler, And
> whoever is intoxicated by it is not wise" Proverbs 20-1,

Drinking is not bad, but getting drunk is. There are so many things we could excuse and justify but, the truth is the truth, right is right, and wrong is wrong, but doing what is right is always a fight climbing uphill, especially if we already have let the weed growth for a long time, and perhaps we are, also blind and deaf, it takes a lot of work, and discipline to change, to get rid of it, not to mention accepting we are wrong, this is the most challenging thing, we might live a lifetime and never know or accepting we were always wrong.

Why would we change if we don't know any better, because we have accepted many wrong behaviors as normal and even perhaps our own social circle sees them as normal too, or perhaps a whole country accepts the wrong in the name of liberty, the truth is still the truth, in Genesis 19, Lot was spare from the destruction of the city of Sodom and Gomorrah, he kept himself to the truth, from this part of the scripture we could learn that, we can oppose to all the wrong in our society and keep our heart and our life in prayer and from all evil that surround us, make our home a small sanctuary, inside your home even if the whole world around you, has forgotten the truth, the eye of the creator is always watching; we are already living difficult times where everything is right and everything is normal in the name of social liberty this should be a warning sign for us, as when things get out of control something big is probably about to happen to restore sanity and unfortunately only when we are suffering and in pain is when we look up and pray, at the city of Sodom and Gomorrah everything was normal and people living there got used to the perversion and evil, this is truth of any city around the world, people inside can get used to any perversion or standards that are actually away from the truth.

And what it's going to happen or where or when or if is going to happen, those questions should be something we should never be concerned about, because all concerns in that regard are a waste of energy, as all of us have one last day, on the day we pass on and leave this world, is either soon, or not too far; what we have to worry is what have we done? To enter the kingdom of heaven Jesus talked about when Jesus told the young guy who was rich to sell everything and follow him, the young guy got sad and walk away, then Jesus told his disciples, how hard is for rich people to get into the kingdom of heaven, but I believe is equally hard for poor people and people in between we are just as bad, and we are, as well, so much attached to everything here in this world, how hard is going to be for all of us, how much harder if we don't get conscious of it, early enough, and make a decision. Why wait? Why no start the relationship with our creator today, to show us where we are wrong, many times we don't even know, because when we think, we are fine, and, you never really did nothing bad at all, you are a good person, we are just too blind with pride, many times we can't see our wrong, it may come in the things we say, the things we do, or the things we don't do, the ones we think, if we don't start reading the scripture and pray, maybe trough prayer slowly our eyes might open, and we might get to see who we really are, who we think we are, and who we really are might be something different, the scripture in the bible is actually the main tool to destroy our blindness, what a great achievement if we ever become transparent, that if anyone read your mind in figure speaking and sees inside your heart, and your behavior when you are alone and nobody is watching, and could see there is not foggy and cloudy thinking, this is so truth as everything we do, say and think, will be accounted for, because the eye of our creator is everywhere, How many of us, don't realize what we say is so important, is just like if we were dragons with fire, every time we open our mouth is just to hurt others, to argue, to fight, to instigate, to promote evil, and even besides our big and loose mouth we might have the perception we are good people.

When so much of what we do is wrongdoing, by our inability to keep our mouth and our mind shot, we need a lot of work, silence is many times our best friend, in the same way, we should silence our thinking, what we think, is always the prelude to our actions, therefore, silencing our mind is a most, when we get caught up thinking something cloudy we should guide the thought to something like the crucifixion of Jesus and think of the pain he endures to save us from certain death, before you know your heart, your mind, and thinking will be heading in a different direction where having good feelings the kind of feelings that are constructive and not those destructive thoughts, as we already might have a life of corrupt thinking we don't need to add more weight to that heavy burden we carry all of our life where we have gotten the results of our corrupt thinking and we are seating on them and enjoying the fruit of our harvest, if we have peace, joy, harmony, and love it is the result of our own doing, but if we don't we need to work on ourselves as the most fierce battle is the battle of our own will, the enemy of every one of us is lying inside every one of us, when you conquer yourself the rest is easier when you read the psalms, protection from the enemy is mention many times, this enemy is yourself and within.

I AM A CANCER SURVIVOR

I feel blessed, I was able to overcome a disease that for certain was going to kill me and certainly was a death sentence if I didn't start treatment early enough, if I hadn't discovered it, late in my life. From early age I started to head toward a direction of reckless behavior, didn't even recognize certain things as wrong like the use of profanity became part of my personality even though I never really did it a home, my mom was the only one who had the privilege, as she was both my mother and my father at the same time she had a lot to handle so she became extra tough to be able to handle a kid like me, and all the circumstances that came her way as a result of been a single mom, she work hard and handle everything as many single mothers do, they are true heroes as they can cook a meal with anything, when there is not much in the kitchen, my mental disease came without even knowing, slowly filling my everyday life and not showing signs until it was deep in my adulthood, spending a lot of time in my youth with kids like me, who had a lot of time and a lot of liberty slowly brought me to a roller-coaster of adventures and little did I know my spirit was getting corrupt in such a way that is so difficult to distinguish right and wrong as if we enjoy, in the name of fun it was ok, eventually I started liking girls and with that attraction came that urge to hang out with them with just one purpose have sex, but this urge to have sex didn't happen because I was young or because I was a teenager, it grow in me gradually without noticing, when another kid at some point in my middle school life gave me a playboy magazine or some magazine of that nature, I became in love with this type of magazines eventually all sorts of magazines of that kind we started to trade, my mind open a door that would be very difficult to ever shot down and to cure this madness, and with all of this, masturbation was very normal, for all of us kids during those times, when we were at school, many times we talked about it and we never really thought nothing bad about it, but the real true of this evil is the inability to love anymore as you see women as objects of pleasure, and nothing else, when eventually the internet made its way in to everyone's home, porn was so easy and readily available as you please, without knowing I was one more of millions of people who think this behavior is normal as it "helps to have better sexual relationships" but the real colors of this monster are everywhere in our society when promiscuity is seen everywhere, but in reality is a disease, a terrible spiritual cancer.

killing the ability to love and respect, the degradation of values, the inability to see a woman as who she really is, when you are watching porn you are simply becoming a slave of perversion, as you would not be able to give your full attention and all your life to your partner, as sooner or later you would always be fantasizing about more women as your mind is already too corrupt, and the sad part of it all, is that you would never be satisfied, this is where so much cheating, so many broken hearts, so many sexually transmitted diseases, so many unwanted kids come to this world, so many abortions, so many families broken it is a real true monster with seven heads and we see it as harmless as having venomous snake as a pet, eventually one day will bite, and you might die, if you are watching porn or if you already are a slave of it, I can assure you, you can definitely get out of that addiction, you can leave your life without it, it is someone who was a slave of this monster who affirms it, you can quit forever, there was a time in my life I thought I would die with this addiction as I knew I didn't have the strength to even contemplating quitting it became a dark secret, but the day this snake bite is the day something big from the nature of the bite destroy your life it is only a matter of time.

When I was a teenager it was cool to have a lot of girlfriends, the more girls you know, the coolest you became, your friends would admire you, but in the back of our mind there was only one objective, this twisted behavior was how the devil poison our soul and it is around and everywhere, and it had poison so much our society, that not only those tentacles have reach men but women just the same, as you could see how much promiscuity there is, as women are not different, the indecent way many women dress today, they lack of modesty in the way they dress, like if they are in need of so much attention, they need to show it all, social media is like a slide show of perversion, and if you are not be careful you can become trap in the many small innocent video or the small innocent picture, women have adopted some gym clothing as a regular everyday dressing exposing with disregard their bodies so hungry for attention so hungry they fill the internet with picture after picture and not remorse at all, plain instruments used consciously or unconsciously to sin by awaking perverse thoughts, please women understand for every bad thought you inspire because of the way you dress and act, you will give account to the creator.

> *Jesus said to his disciples: "Things that cause people to stumble are bound to come, but woe to anyone through whom they come. It would be better for them to be thrown in to the sea with a millstone tied around their neck than to cause one of these little ones to stumble. Luke 17:1-2*

we would all have to give an account of all the acts that lead to a domino effect of corruption, is like if I stage a trap like a spider web, and someone falls in it, I would have to give account to that, but now is all ok, nobody seems to care and nobody says nothing about the indecent behavior anymore, is all normal, many experts encourage pornography perhaps they don't realize how much damage causes to the mind, the heart and spirit, now I know for certain it is not healthy, and the Lord is suffering as the way we have lived our lives, but as always, we are free to choose all the time, but certainly we not always choose wisely, for five minutes of stupidity an eternity of torment.

> *Flee from sexual immorality. Every other sin a person commits is outside the body, but the sexually immoral person sins against his own body. Or do you not know that your body*

is the temple of the Holy Spirit who is in you, whom you have
from God, and you are not your own? 1Corinthians 6:18-19

Everything starts at home, we as parents have a huge responsibility, the entire life of our kids is on the line, what they do or they don't is in direct proportion on how much we got involved in their life and their decisions, it is impossible to be right behind them all the time but we should always have a closed relation with them as much as possible, but the most important thing is to feed them with the word of God, if we don't someone somewhere eventually will, right or wrong information will be the base and the footings for their future behavior, what they see is what they learn, if our faith is weak, if we don't believe in Jesus they probably won't either, our kids are a true reflection of us, if we smoke chances are they will too, as with so many other things we do or we don't; but the faith and the knowledge of a spiritual God who came to the world as a men, to redeem the world, to give us back what our ancestors lost, those ancestors who we all come from, disobeyed when they ate from the forbidden three, unfortunately we are still paying, with all the struggle, with all the hard work and never ending Problems as we are at the hands of the enemy, this spiritual God who told us:

Jesus answered, "I am the way and the truth and the life.
No one comes to the Father except through me. John 14:6

This Jesus who could turn our lives into a heaven on earth, by giving us his peace a peace only Jesus can give a peace that detaches your hearth from this material world, this Jesus who made so many promises to all who believe in him and follow him, this Jesus who claims to be God and prove it in so many ways is the one who can help us raise our kids properly and take them away from all the traps that the enemy has set for them and us, this Jesus is the one we push aside, this Jesus is the one we ignore, this Jesus is the one who we give our back, but we only remember when we are in trouble, and then we ask for help, why is so hard to trust Jesus? Because we are unable to understand we are, a living spirit, not just a man, a spirit after we are men, and the almighty God is spirit, why don't we start fighting back with all the weapons God gave us for the sake of our children, for the sake of our own eternal life, we could feed our kids with all the secrets Jesus uncover for our salvation, we can help them but if we don't believe and we lack faith, how can we help? if we are lost the same way I was for my entire life, Paul the apostle gave us advice on the way we can fight, the way we should fight,

> *Stand therefore, having fastened on the belt of truth, and having put on the breastplate of righteousness, and, as shoes for your feet, having put on the readiness given by the gospel of peace. In all circumstances take up the shield of faith, with which you can extinguish all the flaming darts of the evil one; and take the helmet of salvation, and the sword of the Spirit, which is the word of God, praying at all times in the Spirit, with all prayer and supplication. To that end, keep alert with all perseverance, making supplication for all the saints, Ephesians 6:14-18*

Why do we feed and dress our kids and shelter them but are unable to feed their spirit, when the enemy comes this spirit is weak and empty but hungry for any food, and this is where the enemy takes advantage, comes feeds the spirit with poison and then, you wonder why your kids are immune to pain, their heart is numb, they lack respect, they are lost, full of spiritual ignorance but deep inside lonely, empty and in many cases feeling hate and repulsion for anything good they believe a little of anything or nothing at all, this way making Jesus a liar and go against Christianity it comes just natural in them as something else is feeding the hungry spirit, but you are too busy worrying about their new cell, or their new games or their cars, when are we going to stop being so obtuse? our main responsibility is neglected and our ruin is certain. Thousands of teenagers are committing suicide; Teen suicide increased 32% in the past four years from 8.4 to 11.1 deaths per 100,000 adolescents ages 15-19, and yet we are neglecting due to spiritual ignorance.

You have these weapons, have you used them yet? Have you taken practice? Are you even in this army?

Why we refuse this help and instead we opt for raising kids without God there are many different ways to help our kids but we put aside the one way who could bring them all sorts of blessings and protection, from becoming drug addicts, alcohol addicts, useless internet addicts, and any other harm that may come their way and corrupt their mind forever, the word of God and his grace is the medicine that cure my cancer and like any cancer survivor I most take my medicine until the last day I live my life in this beautiful creation we call earth, I know Jesus is real, how do I know? is the way he has touch me, his promises; is like when your kid does not behave and doesn't want to learn at school, and you tell him if you behave and start learning I will buy you the ultimate game console or an apple computer and the kid at the end of the year did behaved and learned, he most definitely earn his prize, this is the prize I want, even thou I started mid-year to behave and learn, we all have the chance to earn the price of an eternal life with the king, Jesus told his disciples, is very difficult to get in the kingdom of heaven, how is it difficult? Only if we don't believe, if we don't behave, and if we don't begin to bear fruit.

Jesus is still medicine to heal all kinds of cancer, but a medicine we never look up for and is so easily available, and yet the most powerful, we underestimate, what a life changer is to get to know him, but we go on with our everyday life, people suffering all kinds, of mental illness, depression, sadness, bitterness, anger, and loneliness, the world is in so much need for this medicine but we rather look up for temporary relief with all kinds of drugs legal and illegal, and the people in our everyday lives are like a cooking pressure pot, waiting for the right moment to blow up, if we fear we buy a gun, if we feel empty, we get drugs and live a reckless life, to forget the present for a moment, if we are angry we want to get even, we are in so much need for true medicine and yet we forget there is one since after all, it was about two thousand years ago, this medicine started to be available and all those who took it by heart were never disappointed:

> *And the dust returns to the ground it came from, and the spirit Returns to God who gave it. Ecclesiastes 12:7*
> *But you have come to Mount Zion and to the city of the living God, the heavenly Jerusalem, and to innumerable angels in festal gathering, and to the assembly of the firstborn who are enrolled in heaven, and to God, the judge of all, <u>and to the spirits of the righteous made perfect</u>, Hebrews12:22*

The spirits of the righteous in heaven in an eternal festal life without work, pain or suffering, living a life full of joy, pure and real joy in the presence of our creator it is a promise we could look forward to, it is a gift that was stolen from the disobedience of our ancestors Adam and Eva, but after Jesus came and gave us freedom to go back to the father if we follow the words of his son, this beautiful promise is for everyone and is real, the enemy of God is always at work trying to deceive us all, and he'll never stop working as the end of his time is near, the more people he can recruit to his army the more harm he does to God, as our creator love us all and wishes everyone to believe in his son and in his word, to be save, protected by his powerful arm, and all we have to do is live our lives according to the word of God, read and learn the scripture as to understand a little how our good Lord interact with men and what does he want from each and every one of us, is like if the bible has a unique and single message for everyone, long time ago I used to see bibles here and there and I somehow always thought that book was very difficult to read and understand, I figure you need to be an expert and I didn't consider myself an expert so I rejected it, all my life, little did I know the bible is a blueprint for life, it is a book with so much wisdom for all times and ages, where slowly starts opening the doors to the truth, the only truth that there is, everything else is a partial truth, a supposition or a lie, for those who don't want to believe any reason is good for not to believe, for many of us any reason is good to believe, I use to believe without faith but now I believe because of many personal experiences to the presence of God, the way he has manifest, in my life by touching my heart, I know Jesus is real, and he promises he would be with us until the end of times, I learn prayer is the way to call him, we cannot expect to receive everything we ask for, as many of us don't really know what we ask for, but our Lord knows exactly what we need and when we need it, if we keep up in prayer disregarding if our prayers are answer or not, accepting suffering I'm nobody to preach to anyone, I'm nobody to teach, this is just my personal experience, I don't consider myself an expert in religion matter, it is just my humble experience and how Jesus work miracles in me, all of us grow one way or the other, maybe a few minutes before death or a few years before, I am happy to believe in his promise, I have a long way to go, I hope the good God have mercy on my soul, I don't believe I reach the goal to be there with him, I work every day some days are more difficult than others, sometimes I stumble, some others I feel my prayers crash with the walls and don't reach anywhere, I know for experience is not easy, especially when we face disappointment, and many grievances but one way to get back on my feet is to realize how many other people are struggling for a piece of bread, how many are fighting for their lives at a hospital, how many are lock up in jail with lack of freedom, how many are running from persecution, how many don't have a roof, how many don't have anything, how many people are in the world with real problems and here I am like a spoil kid when his ice cream falls off the table with a tantrum or when one of my toys got broken or when they didn't take me to the park, in figure speaking is similar to the situations we see as problems when many suffer with real problems how can I feel sad and depressed, following Jesus is hard but not knowing Jesus is much more difficult, because without Jesus the problems don't have a reason to be, and we are simply with a lost hope, we might fall in to traps that lead us to easy or fake solutions like suicide, revenge, drugs, alcohol, medications to make us numb with Jesus our problems are put on his hands and his will with prayers knowing God is in control of every situation this takes faith and hope a small price with much better results every time, if we have any addiction we need to ask the one who has the power to break all the chains that hold us in the dark, Jesus can't resist a repentant and humiliated heart.

We have to always remember there is people in the world with real problems, there is people in the world with worst problems than those we face, then in the moment, gratitude comes in, we learn and grow a little more, I know like I said before good would always be attacked, we have to be careful and never to think we have reach the ticket to heaven this thinking is arrogant and foolish, out of this behavior comes much difficult trial, always stay humble waiting for mercy upon all of us, as an electrician when I was young I had some bad accidents when I grow so confident I felt I knew everything and I thought, I had electricity under my command, this foolish behavior is dangerous, and I have my share of bad experiences, now a days I immensely respect electricity and I'm very careful, the spiritual life is very similar, I only do little steps at a time, and my race has just started, I hope God grace follow me in my path, until the day I depart, I look forward to the day I die, even when I understand all my actions will be weighted and how much some people love me. But if they believe and trust Jesus we can be certain we will see each other again. Either you believe his word or not.

> *Jesus said to her, "I am the resurrection and the life. The one who believes in me will live, even though they die; And whoever lives and believes in me shall never die. do you believe this?' John11:25-26*

Jesus asks you this same question now. Do you believe this?

CARRYING OUR CROSS

When we go on our everyday lives we find so many hurdles in the way, in many ways shapes, and forms, many of us just get frustrated and curse our miserable life, thinking we could do better we deserve better, many times these situations transform in frustration, anger, resentment, sadness, and emptiness, we never see all of this things as a step to grow, we question the reason like if there was a conspiracy to make our life more difficult than it already is, how do we channel these feelings, how do we deal with all our problems, do we let all of these situations and problems get the best of all of us? Do we feel helpless? I know I did many times, I felt sad, it feels like all my struggles have been a partner on my everyday life, and if I think about how others are more bless or have better luck, because we have the tendency to think the grass is always greener next door, the truth is this all of us have problems but we assume others don't, until the day you hear such person who you thought was blessed had actually a lot more problems than you did, is not a secret all of us have problems, I have a little baby crawling and it makes me sad to think all the problems and hurdles he and all my kids are going to find in life, is a fact, but why does not one teaches us how to deal with problems that in fact are going to come, we as parents hope our kids never face trouble, but that is wishful thinking, we must have the courage to let them know this world is a jungle and those weak in their faith would end up in drugs, in jail, in sick relationships, in fights, in a vicious circle of dysfunctional families all the time, or slaves of so many addictions, or perhaps just prey in the jungle, some would become predators and others prey, the predators are just narcissist, psychopaths, sociopaths as their ego and self-steam is off the charts, with abuse and intolerance as their signature, and yet full of trouble too, we could either raise them to be predators or pray, with not tools to channel problems when they arise, ways to deal with everything that comes our way, not matter what; and the reason is simple we don't even know how to channel the problems our own selves, we just fall in depression, sadness or anger, or perhaps we disconnect our reality somehow with a television or internet for a moment until we come back to real life, and face who we really are.

Jesus gave us answers to all our troubles as he said I am the way, the truth, and the life, we would never find another truth, another way; and any other way is death.

If we teach our kids the truth about what this world is and where we going as the master Jesus told us, they would always have hope no matter what the circumstances are, the worst of any circumstance a man can think is death in any way shape or form to anyone we love or including our death, but if our faith was truth to the message of Jesus we would have the peace to believe his words and we know he is the truth:

> *Do not let your hearts be troubled. You believe in God;*
> *believe in Me as well. In My Father's house are many rooms.*
> *If it were not so, would I have told you that I am going there*
> *to prepare a place for you?... John-14:1-2*

To all our loved ones who believe in Jesus there is a room he prepares for them in his house, if we have faith and believe in his words we would feel happy they are going to a better place with the King of kings, why do we lack so much faith? Why don't believe his words? Why our trust is so weak? The answer is this: you can't love what you don't know, you can't believe because in your heart there is no room for him and his words.

All of our troubles are by illness, financial, emotional or by our own mistakes, all these things are very important, especially our health but there is a better way to cope with our sick body, it is to offer all the pain and sorrow as a sacrifice, either for my sins or my family or for the entire world offenses, this is a humble way to please our Lord as instead of being bitter, complain and ask why? We don't deserve this? and By accepting, we would prove we are fine with his will, just like his servant Job, whom even after losing everything he owned, his richness, his kids, and his health, he blessed the Lord even after his wife was mocking him for his misery after he served God, this is what you get from serving God?, this is true for all of us as in your own house you would find the most criticism, and more hardship words, but deep in his heart Job knew he owes everything to God, everything was just borrowed including his health, when you turn your life to Christ you would find opposition all the time.

> *I have told you all this so that you may have peace in me.*
> *Here on earth you will have many trials and sorrows. But*
> *take heart, because I have overcome the world." John 16:33*

This form of thinking can be applied to everything that is causing us to suffer if we offer every single one of our troubles struggles and hurdles in sacrifice, even when we are having the smallest inconvenience. In my case I know I am in debt with the Lord, as if I was to pay for all my sins, I would need another life, but instead, I get blessings, how can I not feel ashamed and full of gratitude when we have such a lovable Father when I suffer I often think that instead of this little problem I deserve worst, and I know in my heart is true. I know and believe from the heart Jesus paid for all our sins, providing we believe and change for good our whole life. If we give God our suffering in prayer we could instead be working to truly enter that kingdom of heaven, and this pain we offer with love to the omnipotent God, is a much better sacrifice than if we complain, Jesus himself offer his body and soul to the Father as a sacrifice, all of his apostles offer themselves in sacrifice in the name of Jesus; and suffering was always something that is part of Christianity, many died and were tortured for the word of Jesus, for some estrange reason this is how our father reconcile the world, and the devil selfish nature can't understand sacrifice for love and mercy of the souls; God could reconcile it in many different ways but this is how he choose to, as hard as this pill is difficult to swallow, is so true, we might feel is not fair, how some are enjoying and having anything we might probably lack, suffering is a form of reconciliation if we are meek, but if we become rebels, we might not let our lord do his work on us, and we won't make it any better either, if we have not any control of the small things, how can we expect to change anything with a bad attitude, there are so many places in the bible where Jesus made a point on this matter, but instead so many of us have the wrong impression that if we are good Christians everything in our life has to work out just fine as a prize for been believers and followers, but unfortunately this is not always the case, if we get stuck in our learning sure obstacles and problems are to come, how difficult is it to accept this truth, carry with your cross and follow me, this cross is a burden indeed but is a step to a much better life the real-life the eternal life Jesus offer many times, how many of us reject this cross and say no, we accept Jesus but not his cross, even Jesus in the mountain speech told us this truth:

The Beatitudes

2 And he opened his mouth and taught them, saying:

3 "Blessed are the poor in spirit, for theirs is the kingdom of heaven.

4 "Blessed are those who mourn, for they shall be comforted.

5 "Blessed are the meek, for they shall inherit the earth.

6 "Blessed are those who hunger and thirst for righteousness, for they shall be satisfied.

7 "Blessed are the merciful, for they shall receive mercy.

8 "Blessed are the pure in heart, for they shall see God.

9 "Blessed are the peacemakers, for they shall be called sons[a] of God.

10 "Blessed are those who are persecuted for righteousness' sake, for theirs is the kingdom of heaven.

11 "Blessed are you when others revile you and persecute you and utter all kinds of evil against you falsely on my account. 12 Rejoice and be glad, for your reward is great in heaven, for so they persecuted the prophets who were before you. Matthew 5:2-11

We can be sure if we suffer, we would get our prize from our creator, and we can absolutely be certain Jesus did not lie, yes is so nice to enjoy our life with not suffering, full of joy and pleasant things but we have to ask, is this really what Jesus wanted, when we are enjoying we should think about those who suffer, when we are eating we should think about those who are hungry this would help us keep some sanity and stay humble, as everything we do, or enjoy came with authorization from above.

We have the story of the book of Job, to understand a little why sometimes there is not real reason for suffering other than to glorify God, because if we do suffer in the name of the Lord, the devil gets so confused and gets defeated, because he doesn't understand how love works, how someone can be humble even after so much pain, since he is full of pride, full of hate, resentful because he is a looser but sharp enough to tease,

> *"Simon, Simon, Satan has asked to sift all of you as wheat. But I have prayed for you, Simon, that your faith may not fail. And when you have turned back, strengthen your brothers." Luke 22:31-32*

We could learn a lot from this, the devil asks permission to test their faith, but Jesus intervene to help them, Jesus knows how weak we are and he is there to help us, and even as we would like to think of the devil as a rebel without control, we have evidence with Jesus words and with the book of Job he has to get permission before he can do anything if God is playing a chess game, so what? Who are we to judge, he is testing our strength, He is our creator, we enjoy the benefits of his creation, in many ways the universes must follow his rules and this gives me peace, as for us to come into existence, we belong to him because we originated from him and therefore truly bless because we are his possession. The devil only ask permission to interfere in the lives of those who don't belong to him, the ones who belong to him by choice or ignorance, they might probably have a good life for some time as they would probably not be trouble by their master, because when you work for him you make others sin is a chain of corruption, this master I served for many years by choice and ignorance only instigate me to keep sinning, this way I would be offending more our creator, the more we offend god, the more victory for the devil and we become servants of the devil in many ways, as we instigate others to sin and our families would be part of it consciously or unconsciously, for many years we might walk this path and the Lord could patiently wait, for the love and mercy he has on humanity, he would send servants to show us the way back, we might laugh at them, many times we would get angry, and if we read a message from heaven somewhere, we would justify our behavior to tranquilize our conscious, we are very intelligent to justify, to plan our ways to keep doing the wrong and intelligent enough to forget easily whatever is that does not adhere to our plans, our creator is in this fight too, looking for ways to get our attention to lead us back to him, but we always reject his messages over and over, and I often wonder if we die in this circumstances, how terrible our position would be. We have to meditate on these things and have in our minds present the fact we might not have enough time as we think today, we are alive today but tomorrow we might be in paradise, or wouldn't we? Perhaps the love for the souls is the reason many bad people live longer, is a merciful God giving us more time for repentance. Why do we need God? Why do we need to adore him? for one reason, God is the source of all good, health, abundance, love, and all benefits, searching for happiness anywhere else is like looking for water in the desert "is impossible", many people blame God for the evil in this world but he is a gentleman and respects our freedom he would not come uninvited, how would you feel if I come inside your home without your permission? Exactly that is called respect not until we invite him then we would be under his protection and in his love for the souls he is constantly trying to guide us just for the love of humanity he does not need us he loves us, we, on the other hand, are lost and die without God.

Is our duty to pray for those souls who are complete slaves of the world and servants of the enemy, the good Lord had mercy on all of us; one day he called us, and we listened, many others deserve this opportunity, we shall never cease to pray, for those who still don't know Jesus, how sad and terrible not knowing the truth, pray and pray because even if they want to detach from their bad ways, the enemy has some power over this blind souls, and when he knows these souls are awaking he tightens the grip on them. We are obligated for the mercy and the love God had on us when he touched our hearts to return the favor for those who are weak.

When things are going really well and we are in the wrong path, plus the things we are doing are not so good, perhaps bad attitude for life or for others or the way we have lived our life is not something to be proud of, and all of a sudden we get in to a tragedy or all of our life turns south, it may be the mercy of the Lord to make things difficult for us in order to make us humble to understand we have not control, to understand we were walking the path of self-destruction, because is unfortunately many times when we suffer that we look up for help, the good Lord wants us to find him and when our vision is blurry with so much glitter with so many distractions we simply don't have time for God, is in tragedy we start thinking there might be a God somewhere perhaps he can help me, this is why we should never feel jealous for those whose everything in their life's is doing really well even if the way they have lived their lives is questionable, because we don't know where they are heading, unfortunately when things are doing really good many times we don't look for God, is until we suffer we wonder of his existence, and when this adversities happen we don't realize is actually the mercy of God in action because to him our soul is far more precious than all the glitter we are blinded with, this is why adversity in situations like that, are actually the mercy of the Lord even if our mind can't understand, we only see in front of us and our vision of things is very limited, when our life is doing really good we should bless our creator, when things in our life are not going well we should bless our creator too because for certain we never have the steering of everything we do, but if we let him do the steering even when there is obstacles in the way we know we are going to be just fine.

"For I know the plans I have for you," declares the Lord, "plans to prosper you and not to harm you, plans to give you hope and a future." (Jeremiah 29:11)

Paul the apostle told us the Lord desires all man to be saved and to come to the knowledge of the truth; all men to be saved not one soul lost, meaning he is on our side as long as we allow him to help us, we must surrender to him to allow his works take charge in everything we do, not our selfish heart and our one mind direction, that got us in so much trouble since day one.

Thomas had a hard time believing Jesus was alive, he represent all of us who would find it difficult to believe but we have to make use of faith, but if we do follow our internal compass and our heart, read the Gospels this would awake our faith and guide us through the rest of the journey, there is no doubt we are spiritual beings and we will always look for answers in that direction, we were created that way on purpose, to see if even crawling in the dark and through the things we can see and feel, we could find our creator; but even besides all the facts many would never believe, they would even put Jesus words and existence on doubt and even all the books of the bible, as men created, which is true to a certain extent as this books were made by men inspired by the holy spirit, but the nonbeliever would sadly reject these facts, this is sad as the majority of men created have to be tested on faith and love to meet our creator criteria. Pray but not in a selfish way, pray for all the nonbelievers and the sinners and many times this is all about you can do for them, when you are waiting in a line you won't go in until is your turn and not before, is the same with those who are not ready yet, maybe one day they will be touch, but we might help them with our prayers to move faster in the line, we just need a little consideration since most people in the world is good people but many have the wrong information and many are hurting, many are just confused but we are all the same, a heart beating, a mind thinking, family and friends, we are in general looking for the same things some more than others but in fact, we are all brothers and sisters, part of a big family.

Have a conversation with Jesus on the other side of the table invite him to your home and talk just like if you were talking to your husband, your wife or a friend tell him all of your situations, he is there, this is not pretending, God is omnipresent, you could talk in silence empty your heart, ask if you will for those many lost souls and those many in need of his love, this is an act of mercy on your part as this act of kindness won't be forgotten, I say this with certainty because God is with you.

For me, one last messages was direct and scary, I was warned by someone who I never really knew, a nurse I don't recall her name; I used to work at Duke Hospital as an electrician and I saw this woman a few times the same way I meet so many people, I used to talk to so many people,

I would say hi! to many, but this one day was different as she approach with some small talk as I was working nearby, I was happy and joyful that day, but when I was about to leave she said why are you so concern, I was puzzle by this comment, she said I know you are, deep inside I knew many things were trouble me in my head, but I didn't let none of that out, not a signal, then she said I want to tell you something but not here, do you mind if we meet at Starbucks, then she went on to say she has a gift, and sometimes she gets this messages out of nowhere, that she has to communicate to others, she said sometimes I'm walking on the street and I have to tell someone a message, I get out of nowhere, I just do it she said, and people take it however they want, I just have to pass it on, I was surprise and puzzle, when we finally meet after some small talk and very little conversation, she said, this is what I have for you; you need to read the bible from a to z, you need to straighten up your life if you don't, the Lord would turn his back on you, you do what you want I just gave you the message, I was living a double life, so this message pertain to me I knew what she was talking about, I ask her about my business and some other things and she said, I can't see nothing else, I can't get nothing else. I believe her, the message was simple and yet scary my Lord had enough with me and in his infinite mercy he talk to me through someone, it was my choice to discard the message or listen to it, and to say the truth I was very scared, I didn't want to be on the other side of the fence against God, even thou that's where I was.

On the same afternoon, I open the bible for the first time and that is how my journey began, a journey full of hurdles and trouble where the life I once knew was turned upside down, there were many times I wanted to die, it wasn't easy to open up, and show the world who I was, I pray to him, to take me, but I was so naive and ignorant, as I comprehend now, I wasn't aware of what I was asking, because if I die with all my sins on my back, I know now, I would probably be condemned, this is another proof for me, of God mercy, he knows what we need when we need it, but we have to have an open mind and the heart to accept it, the spiritual things don't need logic and the certainty is only faith.

I know perhaps so many take those direct or subliminal messages for nothing or just imagination but God does not talk to us directly, he uses others to correct us, to reprehend us, and to warn us, is really up to you to discard it and keep on going on with the life, but is then when things start spinning out of control, things happen, accidents happen, suddenly we might get some illness, we then have to learn things the hard way, because we might be hard headed, is always best to start searching all the things our conscious is not happy with, and meditate on them to see if we can straighten up, we all know is not easy, is not easy to quit anything we are so used to enjoying, even when we know is harmful; if you grab a glass of dirty water and look at it, we know is gross and disgusting, this is how we look when we dirty, our soul with all the things that are harmful, this things might be physical, psychological or spiritual anything that has cause addictions, anger, depression, sadness, hate, anything that brings sorrow in our life and as we continue we just keep getting more dirt in the glass, until we might become like dirty black oil in the glass, not until we start pouring clean water slowly the dirt starts dissipating and the more clean water we pour the more this glass start to get clean inside, the dirt starts spilling until the clean water takes over again, this isn't fiction is a fact and, what is this clean water?, the word of God, is all the positive things you start feeding your mind with, is always going to work, even when you think is a waste of time to read a good book, the bible, to listen to a good sermon, to listen to an audiobook, to calm your spirit with some good positive music, the nature, a hike, a lake, the ocean, a positive program that lift your spirit, that kind of program that helps you get lifted, exercise, a jog, and forgive, there is just, as many positive things we can do to start pouring that clean water to a better you, but if you really want a water jet, confess your sins, get rid of all hate, start loving more, it will never be easy but if we don't walk we will never get where we want, there is no such thing as something for nothing if we want results we need to take action and follow the master of Galilee.

(Jesus said, For I gave them the words you gave me and they accepted them. They knew with certainty that I came from you, and they believed that you sent me. I pray for them. I am not praying for the world, but for those you have given me, for they are yours. All I have is yours, and all you have is mine. And glory has come to me through them. John 17:8-10)

It's not easy to follow the teachings of Jesus, it will never be, the master was radical in his time, and is even more radical in this modern times, is a challenge and it may even go against everything we dream of, I believe deep in my heart he wants the very best for us even if we might not see it that way, we don't want to suffer at all, we want joy and happiness, but these amazing things are the very things Jesus offers in open arms, the same way he is at the cross, arms open to welcome all of us, and to give everyone who follows him the promise of a big reward. And the most difficult thing is give up our own will, it is the more painful thing we can do, as giving up our will is an internal fight, it might be all of the things that are bad for us and harm us, but we do them because we like them, we enjoy them, for the alcoholic is giving up the drinks, for the drug addict giving up the drugs, for the sex addict, for the porn addict, for the one who eats uncontrollably anything even if we are overweight, for the woman who has another men, or the men who has another woman, like the one who has the habit of talking, gossip and not been able to control and destroys with his or her mouth, for the angry person not getting angry for anything, for the loud filthy language user to keep silence and be respectful, for the liar be truthful, it is very hard to give up our will and do what is right is a fierce battle where our weakness have control of our will and we feel much better if we continue the same, it fulfill our senses and satisfy us; when we were kids we had chores we had to accomplish to have our parents happy, we know for us was very difficult it was against our will, we did it for fear or for responsibility, perhaps we didn't see it right then but we were building responsibility and it was teaching us to be clean to be neat, to be better, discipline is always tough but in the long, it teach us character and transform us in to better much better persons, if we didn't brush our teeth today we would probably be in big trouble but it was a hard habit to learn because at night we were so sleepy, when we got up in the morning for work or school was a hard habit to learn but very well worth the sacrifice, and when we abandon the things that we know deep inside as much as we like them are hurting us, this goes against our will, our will is probably the biggest enemy if is wrongly directed.

Someone who follows the master in spirit and love, does not stop from working, from school, from achieving goals and everything we do, is someone who is at peace, and this peace very difficult is broken as this person transcends beyond of the reality here, knows with certainty everything will pass, sees himself as a simple administrator of all the things he have been trusted with, the home he owns or homes the family, the business and everything, knows inside his soul, he has not ownership and therefor he is free, this peace is the certainty of the eternal life at the place where Jesus dwells, this person has a special happiness nothing in this world can give, sees this world as a blurry dream and hopes one day he would be awaking, is a person who hurts with all the pain and injustice around, and only sees death as a transformation and even if he is not looking forward to it, is at peace with this reality, this person try's over and over again to control the temper, controls and discipline the mouth, discipline all of the senses, and as much as we try, not one person, would ever be perfect, not as long as we are humans, we would never be perfect to the eyes of the creator but the desire the struggle to be perfect, every day our battle field within our own has to start with new ammunition, this ammunition is our prayers and the deeper this are the better we will be prepared.

This is what a warrior is about, what we do with our hands, what we do with what we have, what we do with everything we do, and especially what we do when we have free time, this person knows and realizes we did not come for diversion, we came to this world for learning and growth; the majority of people have the misconception just because someone turns his life into Jesus, now they are Saints and they can't fall anymore but is in the battle when the falls are the hardest and in the battle, the warriors get better and better and in the training, they practice but they are not Saints they are just human soldiers enlisted in Gods army, the word of God is "not for Saints" is for sinners.

> "I have not come to call the righteous but sinners to repentance."
> Luke 5:32

This person looks for true love, one true love, and this love is God and then everyone else falls accordingly in the heart, when we deposit all of our love into a mortal we are in for tremendous suffering, Jesus on the other hand is always there, is reliable and is true love, I'm certain if we were able to meet Jesus we would never be able to love nothing else the same way as the magnitude of his love would penetrate the deepest of our soul, we would never be the same, we would be immerse and full of this love and mercy; craving for this precious love, like a baby, craves for his mother, only when this baby is cuddle around his mother arms he is secure and protected. If we could have the opportunity, is a dream, we are not worthy just yet; if even here in our present life, for a normal individual how difficult would be to meet a president, how much more difficult must be, to be worthy of having a meeting with the author of all existence, there has to be a purification we could probably not be able to accomplish here, but we must strive to earn this maximum honor, although it is written in the scripture, Romans 14-11 and Philippians 2-10 As I live, says the Lord, every knee shall bow to me, and every tongue shall confess to God.

We would get to see him, one way or the other, even if is the first and last, why waste all our life to lose it right there, right then, all of our worst fears would be right then within, knowing how much and how long we reject his true, his word, we going to wish to be here again and do it all again but is already too late. Think and meditate this moment if we were to be there tomorrow, what our situation would be? And if our life was to be exposed as a movie, what would this movie be about? Three x, comedy, action, and fights, criminal, deceive lies, fraud, extortion, pleasure, and gluttony? Or it will be about love, kindness, humility, and all the fruits of the holy ghost, think and think hard, while there is time amend the broken, fix the reap while there is another minute and a whole eternity is at stake, Jesus was always telling this true, is all over the scripture; why are we so blind stubborn and silly, why are we so hard-headed so hard-hearted. Miserable men open your heart and open your eyes; we might not be able to make it tomorrow.

If we try to save our life we will lose it, build a bomb shelter, save tons of money buy more weapons etc. when we go on with our life worrying about our present, and our future, our past, the things we cannot change, the things we have not to control, the world in simple words, we worry too much about this life when only one thing is important, our eternal life with our creator, sacrifice to earn points with all the tools we have to win the prize. Losing our life for all the things we have so much concern and care about, and lose our spirit after we die since we became so corrupt worrying about this life, If we go on trying to save our life from the present moment and from the many things that oppress us thinking we need them, to keep us away from those things we need to care, Jesus told us in many ways nothing in this world is more important than to please God, the rest is secondary, but if we get our priorities upside down the result is disastrous, in our life in general, we would have a whole cloud of darkness, even if we cannot see the dark, is in there. It's very interesting when a disciple told Jesus, master I will follow you wherever you go, and Jesus told him "foxes have holes, and birds of the air have nest, but the son of Men has nowhere to lay his head" Jesus didn't get happy, he just told him the facts, he told him in other words, I have nothing if you want to follow me, go on, but the road ahead is rough, then another one ask "Lord, let me first go and bury my father" and Jesus said "follow me and leave the dead bury their own dead" if we hear this we would certainly think this is cruel and insensible, but Jesus sees the whole picture and knows where the dead father is at, and his family are dead in spirit, because whomever don't accept Jesus as his savior is dead in spirit, even before our physical death; there is no doubt to follow Jesus with the heart is to suffer, in this life, no doubt we will go through many tests and yet we would hear the silence of God in our prayers, when we are in need, there is that silence that chills the bones and make us test our faith, to be or not to be. I remember the Mario game how many obstacles we go through to be able to move on to the next world over and over, this life is not different if today we have peace tomorrow we might be shaken, at the end of the day we have to run to save our life from the many obstacles of every day we have to defeat, don't ever be discouraged, keep on going until your last day if you decide to be on Jesus army expect fierce battles.

Many times over and over we have to prove our faith that little light that help us in the dark while we are in that dark, is our only way out of all of our challenges, because if we have it in our heart we would always find the strength to go on, we definitely don't have a clue about our future, is always uncertain, we could make plans but that is not a warranty to happen when we want, if it ever happens, there might always be plans above for us we might not even know, we always find stories where "if my tire didn't blow up, I would have never met my wife" or "if it wasn't because I got fired from my job I would have never started my business" this stories are always amazing and good remainders, that our father is always working to give us the best there is, but this are the falls as we carry our cross before we get up, and falls are very painful, Jesus fell many times to represent all the capital sins, for us our falls might be perhaps, in direct proportion to the spiritual growth we need at the time.

There is no doubt if we have suffered is because something much better would come out of it, but we would never find the strength inside if we don't have Jesus's hand, something else might give you a hand, someone else might have given you a hand but all of them might be just to get you up and let go where if you are not prepared you might fall even deeper, but Jesus's hand is to get you up and keep you going, nowadays prayer has become a standard in my life, there is the temptation to think is a waste of time, but if we believe the word of Jesus all our prayers are heard by our Father,

> *For the eyes of the Lord are on the righteous and his ears*
> *are attentive to their prayer, but the face of the Lord is against*
> *those who do evil." 1 Peter 3-12*

Trust and faith is the only way to live is really sad to see so many don't even realize what they are losing, the blessings they are missing and the pain they are carrying just because they either don't know Jesus, don't believe, and don't care, and maybe they believe but they see Jesus as far away as the moon, if you need to see a miracle go see yourself in the mirror there is one miracle, all animals in the world survive by instinct, you survived by reasoning, you are capable of creating and destroying, loving or hating, hugging or hitting, you get to choose what to eat, where to work, sleep or not, you choose to marry or stay single, you see, you are completely free a creature with freedom that does not need to be connected to a wire to function or not does it follow one simple goal, like all the rest of the creatures in the world, you are free to choose your destiny and your future, you are an amazing creation in every single aspect and that is a miracle, why the intelligence of any other creature is limited and yours is so vast, is a miracle, why you enjoy comfort, clean water a shelter when the rest of the creatures of this planet struggle every day to survive literally they are at the mercy of predators and the inclemency of the weather and struggle to drink water every single day, struggle to take shelter from the weather but you don't really suffer for survival, is a miracle, what is your privilege? Who are you to poses and dominate this planet and all the creatures in it? Is a miracle, everywhere you look and everything you can think of is a miracle, is a miracle because with all your science and knowledge you would not be able to duplicate one insect or even the leaf of a tree, is a miracle, you want more proof, look deep inside you, all your emotions capable of love, and the rest of them, is a miracle, you still want a miracle look at a pregnant woman how a baby is created and she doesn't even know how it's happening and when the baby is born as a complete human just like you, but do you know? How did it happen? How all the cells form every part of this amazing creature, "computer", "machine", super creation capable of everything, and we call it a human comes into existence, it is a miracle.

If we were to see the deepest of the knowledge in every aspect of this living planet we would go insane is more than we can even comprehend and understand is just beyond our capabilities, is a miracle. Why after we die our body turns to dust and yet we cannot turn that dust into a human or any dust into anything, what holds the Sun and the rest of the starts in a place, why this planet just follows one route forever and ever, is a miracle…

GOD could have created us all good and lucid quickly and made us follow the divine order of things in nature but then we would be no different from a horse, a cow or any animal we have a precious gift, freedom use it wisely...

Life is not difficult, we make it difficult, God's path is not a burden or a heavy load, but a GPS to find the reason and meaning to our life, no matter where you are, the direction is the same for every human on earth...

> "I the Lord search the heart
> and examine the mind,
> to reward each person according to their conduct,
> according to what their deeds deserve."
> Jeremiah 17:10

Printed in the United States
by Baker & Taylor Publisher Services